Step Into Your Miracle Zone

I & gratitude

Cristie Gardner

Step Into Your Miracle Zone

Simple Steps You Can Take To Create Miracles Every Day

Cristie Gardner

POCKET
GARDEN
PRESS

Pocket Garden Press

To my kind, patient, gentle, and super intelligent and inspiring guy Stan. After nearly 49 years of marriage (got married when I was three!), I love you more than ever! Thanks for encouraging me and being an amazing father to our eight incredible humans.

ACKNOWLEDGMENTS

While the phrase *many hands make light work* is true, many hands and hearts and friendships made this book a reality. First and foremost, my thanks to my amazing assistant, Maria Cristina (Tin) Santos. You have been my cheerleader and have been willing to take on any task. Your brilliance is inspiring. You are a genius with design and quick to accomplish assignments. Thank you, my friend!

My deep gratitude to my forever friend, Shirley Smith Ricks, for editing this manuscript in her thorough and expert way. Shirley, high school and university were only just a few years ago, right? Loved you then, love you now.

Leslie Householder and Marnie Pehrson Kuhns inspired, informed, educated, and encouraged me in the graduated level of thinking that is part of this effort. You helped me to make molehills out of mountains in writing this book, and I am grateful to you both. Dear friends Patty Manzano, Jeri Franz, Karen Reilley, Gwen Gibson, Jacque Jennings-Carter, Cari Skrdla, Dawn Norton, Vickie Koernig, Dixie Peterson, and Rena Zaharov—each have lightened my load and lifted my life. Thank you. My gratitude to countless, unnamed friends as well. Each of you know who you are, and hopefully you know the positive influence you have been on me.

To my siblings: Jamie, John, and Melanie—well, let me just say I'm glad we are family. I love you all.

Our children—David, Joel, Josh, Steve, Matthew, Emilie, Caitlin and Nathaniel—each have shown me the incredible power that comes from taking on the impossible.

ACKNOWLEDGMENTS

David: Your support in business and in IT, combined with your expertise and encouragement, gave me the boost I needed.

Joel: Your focus and vision taught me that I can create any desired outcome with persistence (which you have in abundance!).

Josh: Your enthusiasm and thirst for learning and disciplined self-improvement inspired me.

Steve: Your eager, adventuresome spirit and coaching helped me over hurdles and gave me confidence.

Matthew: Your patience, kindness, and knowledge combined with love smoothed the way for me to attain my heart-centered goals.

Emilie: Your entrepreneurial spirit and clarity of thinking showed me a path to follow and gave me courage to follow it.

Caitlin: Your wisdom, empathy, and intuition lighted the path for me, and your loyalty and wisdom lifted my spirits.

Nathaniel: Your zest for life and fearless tackling of both its challenges and opportunities, helped me see possibilities in every situation.

I love you all to the moon and back. And I thank God for you.

*****

Thank you, and congratulations for purchasing this book! My hope is that it serves you, adds light to your life, and helps you get centered in finding and fulfilling your life's purpose(s). Don't get hung up on fulfilling just one purpose; you'll find there are many wonderful things you can do with the amazing gifts YOU have been given. You are the only you in existence, now or ever. Be your best self!

Joy on Purpose was designed to help you find answers and be inspired. If you're caught up in worry, overwhelmed, confused, or discouraged—all of the issues that take away our joy—this book is for you. For example, you'll learn about how you can use the law of opposition, or polarity, to bring your spirits right back up when you're feeling down. You'll learn tips and techniques for talking with your kids—whether they're a teen or a toddler. You'll learn why they have tantrums (sometimes at both of those ages!)

I suggest you read one chapter at a time. They are purposefully shorter and more concise than most chapters. That's so you can read them in between changing diapers or throwing a load of laundry in. And guys, you can learn a lot too! So don't wait to start practicing what you learn in these pages. I hope to hear of your many and frequent successes and epiphanies as you study.

Blessings,
Cristie Gardner

CONTENTS

CONTENTS

CONTENTS

1

Chapter 1: What to Do Now?
The Least You Can Do

We just got back from Boston, Massachusetts, where our youngest son, Nathaniel, received his master's degree from Harvard University. It was an amazing experience. One of the speakers at the commencement delivered such a deeply touching message that I scrambled to take thorough notes so I could share her thoughts with you. The speaker was Lucila Hanane Takjerad, a graduate student. I thank you, Lucila, although you may never read this chapter, for changing my life by sharing your experience.

I think it's safe to say that all of us have days where we doubt ourselves, we're depressed, discouraged, sometimes sick, or overwhelmed. It is during these times that I encourage you—and me—to think about Lucila's message, entitled *"The Least You Can Do."*

Lucila was born in Algeria and grew up as a child in very different and difficult circumstances. As a seven-year-old, she and her little sister had to bathe once a week in the public showers because their home had no running water. Winter nights they cuddled against the cold because the heat was turned off. They saw the worry in their parents' eyes when food was scarce. Their parents reassured them that they themselves were not hungry, when they really were. In 1994 the situation became more serious for Lucila's family when civil war broke out in Algeria. The fear then changed from fear over empty bellies, no heat, and no water, to the fear that they would lose a family member to the war and have an empty chair at their meager table.

One day in 1994, Lucila's life was changed forever. Lucila's mother went to the market place and noticed a chaotic gathering.

Her mother learned that France was offering asylum to families. They needed to write their names on a list from which families would be chosen. Lucila's mother hurried to the table but turned away in despair when asked to write her name. You see, her mother was illiterate, unable to write her name. As she tearfully walked away from hope and possibility, an unknown man ran after her. He offered to write her name–Fadila Takjerad–for her on the list. This man, whom Fadila did not know, performed a simple, single act of kindness. A few months later, through his service, an entire family was offered hope of a better life. And now, twenty-five years later, Fadila's daughter Lucila spoke eloquently as a graduate student at Harvard University.

Tears streamed down my face as I listened to Lucila tell her story. A man whom she never can thank, whose name she does not know, changed the trajectory of her life and her family forever.

Lucila ended her speech with this thought, which I paraphrase. "Of course, we should always do the most we can do. But often the least you can do is the thing most needed."

The Least You Can Do is the thing most needed.

Wow. So there's no need to worry about the huge project we envision, or the massive goal we set? Or the big issues we face? As Lucila, said, "Of course we should do the most we can do, but often the least you can do is the thing most needed."

I have been the grateful recipient of peoples' kindness many times—times when life was more challenging than usual. When we moved to Omaha, Nebraska, for my husband's residency program, a kind neighbor brought over a pan of freshly baked cinnamon rolls and began a lifelong friendship. I never asked her if she had planned on baking rolls for her family that day, and made extra for us, or if she did the most she could do and made a fresh batch just to give away. But the results were the same.

An author took a moment to reply to a letter I wrote to her and began another lifelong friendship. Just knowing her, and sharing ideas with her, is a gift that has changed my life.

My son said to me, *"Mom, you're a classy lady,"* and gave me words of kindness that fed me a feast of self-confidence. Kind friends and clients and family members told me I should be a motivational speaker or encouraged me with their phone calls or texts. The least we can do is often the thing most needed.

So here's your first challenge: Find a small simple thing that is the least you can do today. Maybe it is to sit down with your daughter and give her some cuddling time. Maybe it is to smile at someone who seems downcast. Maybe it is to give a compliment. Maybe it is to greet your spouse with a six-second kiss. Maybe it is to polish a mirror and admire your reflection. Perhaps you can take a nap. Or you can play cars or throw a ball or hug your son. Maybe it is to pay through the drive-up window for the car behind you. Try dancing spontaneously in the kitchen, with the music on loud, to an upbeat song.

One thing I can promise: if you are open to doing the "least you can do," you will find ideas come readily to your mind. And when you say yes and take action, your small act of kindness will create changes that make the world a better place.

I encourage you to do this mindfully. There is a theory called the butterfly effect, which states that a butterfly's wings might create tiny changes in the atmosphere that may ultimately alter the path of a tornado or delay, accelerate, or even prevent the occurrence of a tornado in another location.

In this case, I think we can say that Fadila's benefactor created a butterfly effect that was tremendous for Lucila's family. And looking ahead, we have no idea how much that small act of kindness will change the world. I hope to learn more about Lucila as she goes forward in her life.

So there you have it. I'd like to share a little verse I wrote about the butterfly effect, only this time it is about the ripples in water.

Reflections
by Cristie Gardner
One drop falls in a lakeside pool,
A single drop, and then,
Around that drop a circle forms,
Then round that, one again.
And further out, continuing,
The ripples echo on—
Beyond what we can see, long past
The time the drop is gone.
One person serves another,
In one small, simple deed.
That person's influence expands
To meet another's need.
Then further out, continuing,
Another's vision grows
Extending influence beyond
The people that she knows.
And on and on the circle grows,
Enlarging ever on
Beyond what we can see—long past the time
Our effort's gone.
You cannot see the lives you change
With small and simple things
When love and service ripple on
And give our kindness wings.

Chapter 2: Ourselves, As We Really Are

I don't really think we have just one purpose. I think our purposes change as we grow and learn, as we create new goals and dreams, and as we go through different seasons and situations in our lives. When I speak of a life "on purpose," I really am talking about living deliberately and making choices to get us where we want to go. We'll talk more about that in this and future chapters.

You know, it's kind of vulnerable, getting your voice out there, and I'll be honest, it's a little scary.

To start this whole thing, I'd like you to take a minute and imagine if you were to find yourself suddenly on a different planet. You are able to breathe and survive, but you are surrounded by unfamiliar beings and experiences. People babble at you in a language that you don't understand. And you cannot communicate your needs in words but must cry out or try to gesture when you are hungry or feeling fear or confusion. Then there's dealing with the challenge that your body doesn't work the way you're used to because there's gravity and muscles and weather, and you don't feel like you have control over anything.

If you think about the infinite differences that each of us has in our past, the experiences we've had, our perspectives, our unique talents, the way we look at things, our frame of reference, we might compare it to each of us being on a different planet. And if you add to that the fact that we're all on this same planet, but we—because of our past, our experiences, our differences, our perspectives—give different meaning to words than other people do. All you need to do to find that out is to look in a thesaurus or a dictionary and read about homonyms, synonyms, and antonyms and understand that everybody assigns a different frame of reference to different words.

So in essence, we're all like infants, and William Wordsworth really did a great job describing the forgetting that we experience. He said,

Our birth is but a sleep and a forgetting:
The Soul that rises with us, our life's Star,
Hath had elsewhere its setting,
And cometh from afar:
Not in entire forgetfulness,
And not in utter nakedness,
But trailing clouds of glory do we come
From God, who is our home:/Heaven lies about us in our infancy!

We don't see ourselves as we really are because we all are very different, and it's like we have something similar to a disappearing cloak over us, such as Harry Potter has in his stories.

I'm going to tell you another story that I think is really fascinating.

In Thailand, there is in the temple of Wat Traimit a statue called the Golden Buddha. This statue, for over 200 years, was covered with a layer of stucco and colored glass, and nobody knew what was inside the statue. It weighs five and a half tons. The statue was probably built, they think, around the 13th and 14th centuries. It was moved to a different place, and then for some reason, it was covered with a thick layer of stucco, and the glass. Experts think that it was to protect the kingdom and the statue from Burmese invaders in the 1700s. But the statue remained among the ruins of that city without attracting much attention at all. And then later it was brought—still covered with stucco—and put under a simple tin roof that was dripping and didn't make the statue anything of value—nobody seemed to pay any attention to it until 1955.

In 1955 a new building was built at a temple to house the statue. The statue was moved on the 25th of May, and while being lifted from its pedestal, the ropes broke and the statue fell to the ground. Some of the plaster coating, the stucco, the cement chipped off in the fall, and it allowed a gold surface underneath to be seen. Immediately, as you might guess, there was tremendous interest in what had happened. As they further examined the statue, they realized that inside this stucco and colored glass exterior was a fully solid gold Buddha. In today's value, the gold in that statue is estimated at around $250 million dollars.

I think in this true story is a really great analogy to each of us. You know, we come to earth like Wordsworth said, trailing clouds of glory, and all you need to do is look into a baby's eyes to see the glory that is in them—the light, the joy, the openness. And as we get older, we sometimes create a shield, maybe to hide ourselves from vulnerability. Perhaps we allow a cast—excess weight, or some kind of a protection in an attempt to keep ourselves from being hurt.

Whatever it is, my hope for us is that we start to remember who we really are, and we rediscover the true value that each of us has just in being here. We search for, and find, the ones that we can love and help and serve by loving and helping and serving ourselves. I think we do ourselves a disservice when we minimize our value, don't understand our worth, and forget who we really are.

C. S. Lewis made a comment in one of his books that means so much to me! When I really take time to ponder what he says, it changes the way that I look at the people around me; the people that I don't know, the people that I pass on the street. He wrote:

"It is a serious thing to live in a society of possible gods and goddesses, to remember that the dullest most uninteresting person you can talk to may one day be a creature which, if you saw it now, you would be strongly tempted to worship, or else a horror and a corruption such as you now meet, if at all, only in a nightmare. All day long we are, in some degree helping each other to one or the other of these destinations. It is in the light of these overwhelming possibilities, it is with the awe and the circumspection proper to them, that we should conduct all of our

dealings with one another, all friendships, all loves, all play, all politics. There are no ordinary people. You have never talked to a mere mortal."

And, may I say, you have never been a mere mortal. You have worth that is infinite within you, far greater than the Golden Buddha and far greater than you can even comprehend. And why is that? It's not only because of your thoughts and your inner being and yourself and how you relate to the world, but also because of your potential—the possibility that lies within you, the hope, the dreams, the goals, the talents, the gifts that you have. They make you wealthy in a way that money never can.

So who are you? Well, we're going to spend some time helping you get there, and if you want to be connected with me in future books or podcasts and coaching programs, here's a start.

Write down at least ten of the interests, talents, qualities that make you YOU—your own unique self. Now it goes without saying that there are going to be others that have similar talents, interests, and qualities, but you have a unique combination. Nothing will repeat it, the whole world over, in the eight plus billion people on this planet.

So if you need some help, feel free to ask friends or family—anyone you feel safe asking, but before you do that take some time and sit down with a pen and paper and really be generous with yourself. You don't have to be good at any of the things you write down. You just take a loving assessment of your interests and your dreams, what you love to do, what you want to learn, places you want to see.

Reflections on Becoming
by Cristie Gardner

There's no one who will ever do
The good you do when you are You
And no one who will ever be
As good a Me as I am ME.
The time we march to our own drum
Is when, triumphant, we become.
The moment that we stop and grieve
O'er what we're not, we don't believe.
We each must learn to sing OUR song
And in that moment, we belong
To all of God's humanity—
A symbiotic family
Who focus on our unique gifts;
Where one may build, another lifts,
And each, with talent of our own
Becomes the fruit of seed we've sown.
So, then, go forth, and BE your YOU
And do what God sent YOU to do.
No one can take your unique place
No one can bless with your own grace.
No one can become who YOU are
So shine—and shine YOUR brightest star!

3

Chapter 3: How To Handle Worry

We're going to discuss worry: where it comes from, how it affects us, and what to do about it. First, let me say that if you worry, you're human. Everyone worries. It's a part of our lower brain, our reptilian brain, to worry. We have a stress, or fight or flight part of our reptilian brain that is always on the lookout for the saber-toothed tiger that just might be lurking around the corner, ready to pounce on us. Of course, we know there's not a saber-toothed tiger, but our reptilian brain doesn't really understand that, and its job is to protect us.

So we worry—and our lower brain is *really* good at coming up with things to worry about. Instead of the saber-toothed tiger, our lower brain is going to feed us fears that it thinks we should look out for. Some of the most common fears are fears about our children, health, lack of money, failing, the economy, falling, being in pain, or dying. Even the news can make us worry. Sometimes those fears come with evidence to make us think there is a legitimate reason to worry, allowing those worries and fears (the parent emotion to worry) to paralyze us.

Sometimes you notice a post on Facebook saying, "*Well it's just as we feared! My husband lost his job . . . or I've been diagnosed with this dreaded disease . . . or we lost our home,*" or any other seemingly dire circumstance. Not to minimize those or any other urgent situations. The law of attraction is in effect when we allow our worries to consume us and take over our thoughts; then what we focus on and visualize (even in fear) occurs. That very focus can create unwanted results.

The reality is that WE are creators. WE are the ones who have control over how we handle the circumstances in our lives. We also are the ones who make decisions about what evidence to believe and how to deal with it. No matter how challenging or difficult our circumstances, someone, somewhere, has faced the same or worse situations and chosen to come out on top. When we are discouraged, when we are worried, it is beneficial to read about others who have gone through what we are going through and follow their lead.

As creators, we have the ability to evaluate the issues we are worrying about and choose how to feel, think, and act going forward. As creators, we can take ownership of our brain and choose where to place our focus. We also can be very deliberate, and purposeful, about where we place our energy. We have the power to choose, in any given situation, what our response will be. And what incredible power that is! Victor Frankl, who suffered in the concentration camps and survived the Holocaust, taught us this principle with these insightful words:

"*When we are no longer able to change a situation, we are challenged to change ourselves.*"

"Everything can be taken from a man but one thing: the last of the human freedoms—to choose one's attitude in any given set of circumstances, to choose one's own way."

Faith is the ability to believe in what we cannot see but what is true. Worry is the opposite of faith. It believes in what does not exist, except in our fears. It's like we have bought into an illusion that does not serve us, makes us ill, binds us in fear, causes us to procrastinate, and limits our progress.

All in all, there's really nothing good that comes from worry. Winston Churchill said, *"When I look back on all these worries, I remember the story of the old man who said on his deathbed that he had had a lot of trouble in his life, most of which never happened."*

As parents, our biggest worries seem to come right along with the birth of each child. We worry that they might stop breathing, we worry they might fall and be injured, we worry about stranger danger, we worry about them being bullied at school. The list of possible worries is almost endless. Of course, when our children are small they need our care and protection. It's legitimate to focus on how to protect them, how to meet their needs, and how to help them learn while keeping them from danger.

But as our children grow, so does their need, their right, and their ability to choose for themselves. These are all part of growing up and becoming capable adults. We can aid in this process by allowing them to make choices that do not have dangerous consequences when they are small and staying close and connected with them as they grow older. It's sometimes a huge challenge, but it's SO empowering for them and for us when we allow them their journey.

A client's son was assigned to see an R-rated movie for one of his history classes. He wasn't old enough to be able to see an R-rated movie, and his family had a policy of not seeing R-rated movies. So they expressed their concerns to their son, and together they talked about the pros and cons of doing that assignment. My client and her husband asked him to read the reviews about the movie, and why it was rated R, and then to prayerfully make a decision. They assured him they would honor his decision.

Well, they worried that he would make the wrong choice. In their minds, the wrong choice would be to see the movie. But he was old enough to evaluate the concerns and make his own decision. After exploring his options, he made the choice to see the movie and went. When he got back, his parents asked him his opinion of the movie and listened to his views with respect.

Looking back, that was the best way for them to handle the situation at that time. It cemented a relationship of trust with their son, who was at a vulnerable place in his life. The consequences were manageable, and the experience allowed him to grow in his ability and confidence to make decisions.

Some might say that was a wrong choice. But the worst-case scenario would have been if his parents had mandated his choice and severed or damaged their relationship.

When we worry about others, we are trying to take ownership over their power of choice. On the other hand, when we feel and express faith in their ability to choose wisely, we help them to create a desired, overall beneficial result. And when they make clearly bad choices (which all of us do), we can express confidence in their ability to fix it. That isn't the time for us to jump in and try to be super moms and fix it for them (no matter how much we want to!).

As a teenager, I remember going tubing with some friends. We took inflated inner tubes and floated on them down the river. It was a perfect day, warm sunshine, the river flowed at an easy rate, and we looked down to see the rocks at the bottom of the river. From our perspective, the rocks shone like jewels. It was tempting to jump off the tube and dive into the river and grab some of those beautiful, shiny rocks. So we did. And we'd grab the rocks and hold onto them for a while, until we realized that the rocks were holding us down and making it really hard to surface for air. I didn't want to let go. They were "my" rocks and I had found them and I didn't want to lose my treasures. But at the same time, they were holding me down. And once I got a few of them up out of the water and into the light, they didn't look nearly as enticing. They were just . . . wet rocks.

Worry is like holding onto rocks. We want to gather evidence that our worries are legitimate. They are "our" rocks. They are "our" worries, and the possibility does exist that they might happen. But in the light of an unemotional perspective, using our higher brain, we can see worries for what they are: illusions.

A coach once told me, *"Here's how to deal with worry: Ask yourself, 'Can I do something about this?' If the answer is yes, then do something about it. If the answer is no, release it and let it go.*"

Let go of the rocks. Let go of the worries.

I teach my clients the steps to gain control over worries. So here's your assignment, in ten steps:

1. Write down a list of ALL your worries
2. Prioritize your list and focus only on #1.
3. Be grateful to yourself for "looking out" for you.
4. Analyze the top biggest worry on your list.
5. Is it in the future or is it in the present? If it is in the future, it is an illusion. If it is in the present, take the next step.
6. Inform yourself of the tools you have for solving the worry.
7. Can you take productive action on that item?
8. If it's productive, take action.
9. Acknowledge the worry, but recognize it for what it is.
10. Externalize it: zoom out. Learn from it.

Now you are free from the emotional ties of that worry and you can address the next item on your list.

Churchill said, "*Let our advance worrying become advance thinking and planning.*"

I read of a homeless man whose resources were all gone. He had no home, his car that he had been living in was repossessed, and his hopes were dashed. Then he got an idea. He dressed as nicely as he could, with a long sleeve shirt and tie, and made a sign: "*Homeless. Hungry 4 Success. Take a Resume.*" Then he stood on a street corner and held his sign up.

A passing motorist asked if she could take his picture and posted it on Twitter. It was retweeted more than 50,000 times and liked over 70,000 times. The man received over 200 job offers and now is employed.

"*The solution to any problem is an idea away*," says Leslie Householder. And when you take action, the worry goes away with it. The illusion becomes clear, and you can continue on your journey, unencumbered.

On Worrying
by Cristie Gardner

Let go of all worry
With conscious release
Stay focused; move forward
And feel sweet peace.

4

Chapter 4: The Myth of Perfection

When I was in college, I worked as a "job expeditor" at the computer science center. Computers were a really new thing then—in fact, so new that most people hadn't even heard of them. Way back in 1943, Thomas Watson, the president of IBM, said, "*I think there is a world market for maybe five computers.*"

Well, Tom, I think you were a little off on that one. But I digress. So in our job, we handled the cards that students punched with their code and rubber-banded together the cards into what we called "jobs." We'd accept the jobs at our service counter, remove the rubber bands, and set them in a "can." The contents of the cans were fed into the massive computer. It filled a whole room. Once the jobs "ran"–that is, once they had been fed into the computer and the results printed out on lined paper with holes on each side to feed through the printer, we tore the serrated pages into the appropriate submissions and gave them back to the students. Then we recorded what jobs were completed on a phone message so students could call in to find out if their assignments were ready for them to pick up.

I know this is a bit complex. So stay with me.

On occasion, a loud "DING!" would sound from the computer room, signifying that the computer had shut down. Usually the cause was not intentional, but a bad program submission could stop the whole computing process. Sometimes police would come, because someone had written a malicious program that would cause the printer to go back and print and reprint and reprint the same paper. I guess that was the origin of malware. The malicious programs could damage the whole computer system, from calculations to printers. When that happened, my fellow worker and I had to record the sad news that peoples' homework was not ready and might not be for some time.

My workmate's name was Becky, and we had a lot of fun recording unique messages when time allowed. So Becky and I recorded this message, and the students loved it and called their friends so they could listen to our broadcast (which basically shut down the phone system!).

But here's what we sang, to the tune of the Rice Krispies commercial:

DING! What an awful sound!
Someone's bad program made the system go down.
No programs out, people shout; nothing ran in the can.
Ding! Click and Whirr! Computer!

Well, they thought that was pretty funny, and that was a long introduction, but I think the imagery could prove helpful to us as we think about perfection. In our efforts to write the "perfect" plan for our lives, we make a mistake, and then instead of allowing ourselves to let it go and move on, we rewrite our mental code so that we print and reprint what we did wrong, blaming ourselves, feeling guilt, sometimes even going so far as to damage our internal computer that helps us keep perspective and recognize our worth.

Why is it that when we mess up, we all too often rake ourselves over the coals and feel we have failed?

I believe it is because of the myth of perfection. Many of us turn to the teachings of Jesus in the New Testament and then point to ourselves as we feel a sense of hopelessness about our ability to cope with the challenges we face. But if you read about twenty verses of Matthew, chapter 5, that PRECEDE the commandment to *"be ye therefore perfect, even as your Father in Heaven is perfect,"* you will realize that Jesus is talking about being perfect in love. And love is something we can all do. It's just a continuation of the command to love God and love one another (including loving ourselves). When we love ourselves, we are patient with the learning process that is part of our earthly journey.

Here's that passage in Matthew, if you don't have time to look it up yourself:

Ye have heard that it hath been said, An eye for an eye, and a tooth for a tooth:

But I say unto you, That ye resist not evil: but whosoever shall smite thee on thy right cheek, turn to him the other also.

And if any man will sue thee at the law, and take away thy coat, let him have thy cloak also.

And whosoever shall compel thee to go a mile, go with him twain.

Give to him that asketh thee, and from him that would borrow of thee turn not thou away.

Ye have heard that it hath been said, Thou shalt love thy neighbour, and hate thine enemy.

But I say unto you, Love your enemies, bless them that curse you, do good to them that hate you, and pray for them which despitefully use you, and persecute you;

That ye may be the children of your Father which is in heaven: for he maketh his sun to rise on the evil and on the good, and sendeth rain on the just and on the unjust.

For if ye love them which love you, what reward have ye? do not even the publicans the same?

And if ye salute your brethren only, what do ye more than others? do not even the publicans so?

Be ye therefore perfect [and I'm going to add "in love"], even as your Father which is in heaven is perfect.

When our children were growing up, I read them a book by Madeleine L'Engle titled, *"A Wrinkle in Time."* L'Engle's words and her story are so compelling and instructive! I highly suggest you get a copy and read it . . . and no, the movie does NOT do it justice. Here is a highlight: *"Don't try to comprehend with your mind. Your minds are very limited. Use your intuition."* Those of you who read the book will recall the infamous IT, with the compulsion to make everyone on the planet conform. Children had to bounce balls in perfect unison. Everything was tightly and "perfectly" scheduled, and if someone deviated they were punished. So fear became the motivating factor in obedience.

I think when we are obsessed with attaining the myth of perfection, believing it to be real, we create a fear in ourselves, a sense of panic, because intuitively we know perfection doesn't exist in our present state of development.

When we have children, we watch them as they grow and develop from birth. First their eyes learn to focus, they control the muscles in their neck to move their head, they scoot and then they crawl, and then they walk. Have you ever seen a child give up on their learning process and refuse to try again when they fell the first time? I believe that the urge to grow is divinely instilled within us. It is only as we get older and believe in the myth of perfection that we become discouraged and think we are not capable of trying again.

God is patient with us. We are His children and He loves us! Why would He expect us to become perfect without our having the chance to learn and grow, make mistakes, and figure out new solutions? That is part of the magic of living: We get the opportunity to learn, and grow, and make mistakes, and fail, and come up with better ways, and try again! As my friend Leslie Householder says, *Done is better than perfect.* When we accept the exciting, motivating, inspiring challenge to come up with new ideas, and reframe our experience, and keep going with faith and enthusiasm, we teach ourselves that life is a magnificent journey, with the marvelous opportunity to try and fail and learn and grow and become.

My brilliant nephew is an architect. During his training, his professor was showing him all the "perfect" examples of various types of architecture. And it occurred to Clayton that there was perfection in each of the buildings, but they were, and are, uniquely different. Clayton asked this profound question: *"Do you believe there is an infinite variety within perfection?"*

I remembered that question as I was preparing this chapter, and I contacted Clayton to learn a little more about it. He recalled, *"it was a discussion about the idea of perfection in architecture, but it can be applied in all creative works. Where you can perfect a skill like scales in music or painting or stone carving, there can be a pinnacle of skill. But the variety of outcome when it comes to composition is as infinite as our individuality. So as you perfect your skills, it opens an infinite variety of compositional variability as you work within eternal principles of creation, which are based within geometric and proportional relationships."*

Clayton continued, *"it was to address my concern about maintaining our eternal individuality while becoming more perfect. I don't believe perfection is on a pinpoint or at the top of a pyramid. I believe it's a state of being that when reached enables us to exist in our full potential."*

He's pretty amazing! But then, so is each of us. We are each amazing, children of God, with infinite uniqueness and ability and gifts and experiences, opportunities and interests.

How is it possible to be perfect? You already ARE. You are the perfect YOU. No one can be perfect in being you except yourself. So your privilege is to learn who you are, envision who you want to become, use your intuition, and live into that vision. Most importantly, love yourself enough to recognize that this quest to become you is a lifelong journey, with failures and flub-ups and trying and do-overs, over and over again. But do NOT rake yourself over the coals, because that's part of the process. And do NOT print and reprint and reprint in your memory the failures, but instead keep that vision in your focus. If my intuition is correct, that process continues on even after we leave this earthly existence.

So learn to love yourself, and to be patient with yourself, as you progress along this magnificent journey. The Unitarian Minister Jenkin Lloyd Jones said, *"Life is just like an old time rail journey...delays, sidetracks, smoke, dust, cinders, and jolts, interspersed only occasionally by beautiful vistas and thrilling bursts of speed. The trick is to thank the Lord for letting you have the ride."*

If you want to catch glimpses of perfection, allow yourself the time and the chance to observe the perfection all around you. Notice the sunrise and the sunset. Notice the waves in the ocean, the predictability and order in the planets, the amazing sequence of seasons, and day, and night, the veins in the leaves; the muscles and bones and sinews in your body. But even more importantly, recognize the perfection in your baby's toothless smile, the perfect little hand that clutches yours as you go on walks with your toddler, the perfect delight in your child as she runs toward you with her arms outstretched. Notice the perfection in the hug you share with your spouse, or your dear friend. Notice the perfection in CONNECTION. And stay connected.

What a wonder it is to be experiencing this life here and now, together! So stay connected. It's good to be busy. It's good to be productive. But the greatest perfection we can produce is found within loving ourselves, our God, and each other. So no matter how busy you are, take a minute to make a difference. And savor the perfection in every precious moment.

5

Chapter 5: How to Calm a Tantrum

While walking along the cobblestone sidewalks in Boston, I observed a mother holding her little boy's hand. He looked to be about two years old. They began crossing the street, and he literally danced with enthusiasm as he walked. His hand could barely reach his mom's hand, so when he bounced along it created a tug on her arm. I overheard her say to him, *"It is very inconsiderate for you to bounce. Stop it now."* And she jerked her arm, pulling him along. This mom was having a tough time remembering Childspeak. What two-year-old knows what inconsiderate means? And was he really being inconsiderate, or just being a happy, excited little boy?

This chapter is designed to help you interpret your young child's language (which includes his body language) and to learn the very important language of Childspeak, which really you just have to remember. Everyone has been a child, so everyone knows Childspeak, but when you're a parent and no longer a child, it's hard to remember how children communicate.

As a parent, our job is to brush up on our Childspeak language skills. If you were exposed to another language, such as Chinese or Spanish, as a young child, you have the language inside your head, and it will not take long to relearn it. So we're going to do that with Childspeak. Later we can relearn Teenspeak, so we can adapt the same language and knowledge skills to our teenagers, and even those in between. With a little effort we can translate all of those skills into Spousespeak, which should help us in our relationships. But today, we'll focus on Childspeak.

What this chapter is NOT meant to do, is make you feel guilty. Understand that we are all learning and relearning and remembering. We have to feel patient with ourselves, and our own learning process, so we can learn and relearn the skills to be patient with our little ones and what they are trying to communicate. Then we can be more aware and better meet needs of our growing, not-so-little ones.

Also understand this: No one of us is going to be on top of our game ALL the time. We have days when we feel sick, when we're overwhelmed, when we have a crisis or unanticipated interruption to our schedule, when we just flat-out don't feel like doing much more than grabbing a bowl of our favorite ice cream and watching a mindless game show. When we have been bombarded with several intense or taxing experiences in a row, we can become numb to our children and their attempts to communicate with us. So the purpose of this chapter is to help us raise our awareness, and by doing so we have a better chance of being better next time our toddler has a tantrum. If we understand what they are really saying, we get a chance to listen and respond appropriately, instead of throwing our hands up in the air in defeat, or yelling back, or lapsing into depression.

To begin this ambitious exercise, let's first establish that EVERYONE wants to be successful. Everyone wants to do things "right." We want to please others. We want to be heard, we want to express ourselves, we want to be loved and needed. Our children are not trying to make us angry. They are trying to communicate. They are trying to please us, to do things correctly, and to learn. They haven't really had much time on earth to figure out all the innuendos in communicating. They reflect what they have observed in us and other important people in their life. And beyond that, they have to rely on their very meager vocabularies to express pretty profound thoughts and emotions.

What gets in our way of understanding them is this, and pay attention, because this is key: We assign adult intention to child behavior. Put another way, we project what we are feeling into a motive that we assume the child has lurking in their brain. That's when we need to take a step back, rethink, and figure out what our child is really saying.

We need to own our response and change the story we are telling ourselves about what our child is experiencing and how we choose to respond to it.

Maslow's hierarchy of needs gives us some key insights we can use in recognizing how to connect with our little loved ones.

First and most elemental, we have physiological needs. We need food. We need rest. We need to be able to breathe. We need water. We need clothing. Maslow also included sexual needs, which are necessary for the survival of the species, but since this chapter is about understanding our children, I'm going to assume you have that one covered. Basically, physiological needs refers to a stability in knowing that we are provided for, and that someone is taking care of these most elemental needs.

A little baby is aware of her physiological needs, but her language for communicating is very limited. She can make faces, she can squirm, and she can cry. Parents have to learn what their new baby needs by listening to the confusing communication and then addressing the needs. Sometimes we don't figure out what the baby is "saying" in baby speak, and baby becomes more and more insistent, louder and more demanding. Just remember: baby is NOT trying to irritate you. She is only following her internal system so she can let you, her only provider of her needs, know that something really important is not happening for her! She might need food, she might be having pains in her tummy, she might need to be changed, she might need soothing, or she might be sleepy.

The more quickly, calmly, and thoroughly we understand and handle the basic needs of our baby, the more secure he feels and the calmer he will be. Sometimes as parents we feel like detectives, trying to interpret what baby is saying. It gets easier as we get to know our baby and learn his signals.

A screaming baby does not mean, "*I hate you.*" A screaming baby does not mean, "*I am spoiled and demanding and it's all about me.*" A screaming baby has a basic need that has not been met.

Moving up from physiological needs is the need for safety. We don't worry too much about safety when we are little because we aren't as aware of our surroundings when we are small. Our children are just observing the magic of the world around them and are oblivious to danger.

For example, children are automatically attracted to water. It's fun, it's refreshing, and it's exciting. But children are oblivious to the potential danger in water, so we have to teach them water safety. Until they have learned how to swim, it's important to protect them and keep a close eye on them. One of my clients in California told me what happened in his family: his little boy had been playing quietly in the fenced yard. My client hadn't checked on him for a few minutes, and "something" made him get up and look for his toddler. Somehow his son had gotten the fence open, and walked into the neighbor's yard, and just as my client found him, he was squatted down and leaning over the deep end of the pool. Fortunately my client listened to the "something" that made him check. Not all stories end up happily. But we do our best to keep our children safe.

As we get older, our basic safety needs include financial security, health and wellness, and being safe from accidents and injury. But those typically do not consume our little children's attention. Along with the physiological needs, our security and safety are our basic needs.

Once our basic needs are met, we come to Maslow's next need in the pyramid: social interaction. Little children are just beginning to recognize the fun of friendships. They connect first with family, because family is where they are, or should be, safe. In social interaction, little children are also learning how to control their emotions, and it's easy for them to lash out and hit or push another toddler over.

How do we as parents react when we see our daughter shove or hit another child? Calm is best. Forcing her to say she is sorry doesn't address the core issues. We can help her to learn compassion and empathy through role play. For the moment, an apology can quiet things down, again done with a calm manner. Later, we can talk about what happened, and talk about how to do it differently next time.

The single tool of anticipation is one of the most valuable tools I discovered when raising my family. If you are going to fly somewhere for a vacation, take the time to be relaxed and talk happily about what it will be like. Children can help pack their suitcases. While packing, you can talk about how it will feel when you get in the airplane and see the sky and the houses getting smaller and smaller when the airplane takes off. You can talk about how fun and exciting it is to be up in the clouds. Anticipation creates a taste of the experience so that children are not taken by surprise with unexpected events.

Infants have very small ear canals, and the pressure in take off and flight and landing can cause great pain. That's why so often you hear little ones screaming in an aircraft, and their frantic parents trying to quiet them. If you are a nursing mother, you can try nursing your baby discreetly until the plane has reached cruising altitude. Or an older baby can be given something to suck on.

With social interaction, all of the emotions in children seem to become more intense. Remember, they are new at figuring out big feelings. Their vocabulary may not be equal to the size of the emotions they are trying to express. They might be saying, *"I'm hungry,"* or *"I'm tired and I feel out of control,"* and instead of words it comes out as a tantrum. I have noted, strictly from a professional standpoint, that this happens most frequently when we are in a store with other adults looking on disapprovingly. Ha! And also I have determined that the adults looking on with such disapproval do not have children of their own. Or they have dementia and can't remember that their perfect child also had tantrums.

What are some of the other things that children are saying when they erupt suddenly into screaming fits? They are saying things such as, *"I don't like myself right now, but I can't control my feelings." "I have this huge need and I'm trying to tell you about it but I don't have words." "I need a nap and you dragged me into this store and I can't handle how tired I am."*

How is the best way to handle a tantrum? With love and with calm. The second a child starts to act up, our parent radar needs to pick up the cues so we can go into super calm mode. We pay attention to the child, right then! and get down on their level so we can calmly talk and ask questions. "You sound sad. Are you hungry? Are you tired?" If you're in a grocery store, get a package of acceptable quick food and feed your child. You can pay for an opened box, just as well as a sealed one. Keep snacks available in the car so you don't get caught unawares.

A client called me a few weeks ago and tearfully said, *"I don't know what's wrong, but I just feel so sad and lonely."* I asked a few questions and she admitted she had not eaten breakfast yet that day. Immediately I suggested she get some food in her mouth and within minutes she was laughing and cheerful. Our bodies need fuel. Our kids' bodies need fuel, especially when their active little selves are running around playing outside. And if a grown woman doesn't always recognize the cause of her despair, how's a kid to know?

When we react with calm to a child's tantrum, we immediately deescalate the crisis. It's almost like we are the negotiator in a hostage situation. A negotiator has to figure out what the demands are and how to meet those demands without compromising safety. That is exactly how to handle an out-of-control child. Calm, connection, comfort, and cuddling.

It goes almost without saying that an ounce of prevention is worth a pound of cure. The more you can anticipate the difficult situations ahead, the better you can be ready with patience, calm, love, and understanding. Snacks, water, spare diapers, and band-aids are always good to have on hand.

Another truly effective tool I used with my little children was role play. We practiced what to do and say before social events and after times that caught us off guard. How would we do things differently if we could do them over again? Talking safely, calmly, and lovingly about those helps tremendously with keeping the children happy and secure.

One of my clients was concerned because her little boy always seemed to wake up crying. The solution she created was to walk into his room with a happy smile and say, "*It's a beautiful day!*" As soon as he began to talk he would wake up saying, "*Bootiful day!*"

I want to reiterate the two things to be aware of as we help our children develop a more stable, consistent emotional state:

First: Remember that your child does not have a hidden agenda. Remember to own your own feelings and not assign adult intention to child behavior. If you must project anything, project happiness to your child. Project confidence in your child's ability to solve problems (and remember to be age-appropriate when you talk to them). Take a step back, rethink, and figure out what your child is really saying.

We need to own our response and change the story we are telling ourselves about what our child is experiencing and how we choose to respond to it.

Second: Constantly help your child to anticipate experiences, circumstances, and scenarios. You will find that when they have been introduced to what is going to happen, even if things don't go exactly the way you think, the anticipation will help them keep calm when they are in the midst of the storm.

Raising little ones is SUCH a big job! It's easy to be tough on ourselves when we have a rough day. But keep going, and keep changing your thinking until you can reflect happiness and confidence in your ability to interact with love, calm, and patience.

Life with kids is a busy time. But every effort you give makes a difference. So no matter how busy you are, take a minute to make a difference.

Chapter 6: Accomplishing Your Quest

When my husband and I met, I was dazzled by his exceptional tennis skills. On top of that, he was an excellent student and he played the piano. On our first date, he played "Clair de Lune," for me, and I melted right then and there. His tennis prowess paid for his university education, as he was the number one player for four years. He still loves the sport and watches the top matches whenever he can.

Novak Djokovic and Roger Federer played in the finals at Wimbledon, and we had fun watching the match. I have to confess, I'm a Federer fan and was a bit disappointed that Djokovic won in an unprecedented tiebreaker after a riveting several hours of competition. But I became a fan of Djokovic too when I listened to the interview he gave after the match. This is what he said:

"I remember as a kid, I was improvising and making little trophies out of different materials and going in front of the mirror, lifting the trophies and saying 'Nole [Novak] was the champion!'"

— Novak Djokovic

My husband turned to me and said, "*and that's what your next chapter is about!*" I love it. He was right. It resonated so much with me that I had to share Djokovic's story, as well as a few others, to inspire myself and my listeners to achieve our dreams.

What is Djokovic's secret? He literally created his success in his mind, in his spirit, in his heart, long before it came into being. The part I love best about his success is that he created his own trophies, out of whatever he had, so he could envision the experience and grow into that vision.

Along the way, Novak Djokovic had to practice, practice, practice, and spend countless years of effort to become the tennis player he dreamed of being. But the vision was set in his heart, and he needed to live into his vision, being willing to pay the cost in terms of commitment, persistence, and consistency.

Djokovic also thanked his parents and his family for their support and sacrifice to help him accomplish his dream. He literally realized the promise made by William Hutchison Murray:

"*Until one is committed, there is hesitancy, the chance to draw back, always ineffectiveness. Concerning all acts of initiative (and creation), there is one elementary truth, the ignorance of which kills countless ideas and splendid plans: that the moment one definitely commits oneself, then Providence moves too. All sorts of things occur to help one that would never otherwise have occurred. A whole stream of events issues from the decision, raising in one's favour all manner of unforeseen incidents and meetings and material assistance, which no man could have dreamt would have come his way. I have learned a deep respect for one of Goethe's couplets:*

> *Whatever you can do, or dream you can, begin it.*
> *Boldness has genius, power, and magic in it!"*

Djokovic dreamed it, committed to it, did not hesitate, and the results were a world championship ranking in tennis: his dream.

In preparing this chapter, I had the pleasure of studying the experiences of so many great people who dreamed and achieved! Some of them are alive today, and others lived lives of commitment that began incredible legacies we can see years later. But all of them have a common theme. They envisioned the results they wanted, and they persisted until they achieved their desired results. For example:

J. K. Rowling was as poor as someone could be in today's Britain without reaching a state of homelessness. Her marriage had disintegrated, she had a daughter to care for, and all she had was hope, her story idea, and her typewriter. Her efforts had ended in failure, but failure didn't break her. On the contrary, failure helped her discover who she was. Rowling says,

Failure gave me an inner security that I had never attained by passing examinations. Failure taught me things about myself that I could have learned no other way.

And as a result of her failure, and trying again, the whole wonderful Harry Potter series was born.

Reverend Martin Luther King's inspired message began a movement that continues on today. In one part, he said, "*I have a dream that my four little children will one day live in a nation where they will not be judged by the color of their skin but by the content of their character."*

Oprah Winfrey grew up in poverty. She was sexually abused as a child, ran away from home, and gave birth at age 14 to a baby girl, who died after only two weeks of life. Her first boss told her she was too emotional to be successful in television. But she persisted in following her commitment. Oprah said:

"People refer to me as a brand now—the Oprah brand. I never knew what a brand was when I first started out. I became a brand by making every decision flow from the truth of myself. Every choice I made, for every show that was going to be on air, I made based upon 'does this feel right?' 'is this gonna help somebody?"

Emily Blunt, the famous actress who just recently played Mary Poppins in the sequel, once had a stutter that she could not overcome. She practiced saying funny things in different accents, which helped her overcome the stutter. But she was bullied and teased as a child for her stuttering. Her vision of acting came about because of her commitment to overcome a handicap.

Each of these people, and countless others whose stories fascinate me, persisted with commitment and vision to achieve their dreams.

How do we achieve our dreams? I have to confess, some of my dreams are not things I want to achieve. Those can happen when we eat too much of the wrong things before going to sleep, or we have too much bubbling around in our brains to stay focused on our most important objectives. But the message I have for you is that you CAN achieve your dreams. You can follow specific laws that are in place and your dreams will happen for you. As Walt Disney, another dream achiever whose story lives on, once said, *"It's kind of fun to do the impossible."* And no matter how impossible your dream is, someone, somewhere, has faced similar or more difficult circumstances than you have and triumphed. You can do the impossible.

So let's talk about how that's done.

The first step, and the most important one, is to know what you want. I mean, you really have to know what you want, and you have to be very specific. God showed us the way to make that happen with the creation of this earth, and all of the animals and people upon it. He envisioned everything in detail and spoke clearly about the desired results. You can reread it in Genesis.

Create your vision on paper, written in ink with your own hand. Don't just type it. Writing it down gets it into a more visceral place, where you can feel that desire within your heart. Get very specific. You want a wonderful relationship? What does that look like? Different surroundings? Where? How will you know you have achieved your dream if you don't know what your dream looks like? So meditate on it. Spend some time visualizing, with no limits. How do you want to look? How do you want to feel? What do you want to accomplish? What does your perfect day look like?

You can work on this for a while and let your brain play with possibility. Once you set your intention, you can let your brain and spirit take over, and ways will begin to open up for you to attain your desired result. This is the main law for success that is not easy to discover. The more specific you are, and the better you visualize, the more material your brain and spirit have to work with, and they can set about accomplishing your goal even before you can begin taking action.

Gail Miller said, "*There is a higher power always watching over you and ready to help you. Day in and day out, be consistent with your efforts. If you have a goal and you want to get there, you have to do something about it. You have to make a plan and then day after day adhere to your plan.*"

"*Do not wait; the time will never be 'just right.' Start where you stand, and work with whatever tools you may have at your command, and better tools will be found as you go along.*" —George Herbert

Men and women who move forward with commitment and faith will see miracles happen. I have seen them in my life, many times. Once you have committed, and know what you truly desire, set to work, and have faith. Boyd K. Packer said:

There are two kinds of faith. One of them functions ordinarily in the life of every soul. It is the kind of faith born by experience; it gives us certainty that a new day will dawn. . . . It is the kind of faith that relates us with confidence to that which is scheduled to happen. . . . There is another kind of faith, rare indeed. This is the kind of faith that causes things to happen. It is the kind of faith that is worthy and prepared and unyielding, and it calls forth things that otherwise would not be. It is the kind of faith that moves people. It is the kind of faith that sometimes moves things. . . . It is a marvelous, even a transcendent, power, a power as real and as invisible as electricity. Directed and channeled, it has great effect.

This week, take however long it takes to think about, and dream about, the results you want in your life. Then write it down, as detailed and specific as you can be. Don't worry about HOW it's going to happen. Just put it out there and have faith, and work with commitment to get going on it. On the way, you'll notice some delightful sidetracks and you'll see that a greater Force is guiding your steps toward your ultimate dream come true.

In creating this chapter, I wrote a poem to inspire you folks who may have placed others' dreams above your own, and you're wondering if it's too late for you to achieve yours. Know this: it is never too late. It is always EXACTLY the right time. Begin and continue and it will happen. My poem is called "The Daughter's Quest," but it can very much apply to men as well:

The Daughter's Quest
by Cristie Gardner

Her vision helps her see the goal;
Though far beyond the distant knoll.
Her faith believes results will be
Her own potentiality.
But all will not flow as she seeks;
It may take time in years or weeks.
Her efforts may be spent in pain,
Refining fire or cruelest rain.

Still resolute, she stays the course
Her labor sure, with no remorse
A woman centered, holding fast
Will seek her visions of the past
And then become, in strength and calm
Creator of her faithful psalm.
No, she is not a perfect soul
But through her vision and her goal,
She focuses on what can be,
And thus fashions eternity.

Remember, every effort you give makes a difference. It is sometimes through accomplishing our goals and dreams that we inspire or help others to accomplish theirs.

Chapter 7: How to Change Your Perspective and Perceptions

A couple of months ago, my husband and I joined two of our sons and their families in popular Lake Powell in Utah. We had so much fun visiting, relaxing, meditating, hiking, and of course, water skiing. The trend nowadays is to wake surf, and my hubby wanted to give it a try. After four face plants, he got up and enjoyed a really great time surfing the wake.

But over the course of the next four weeks, he noticed some changes in his eyesight. His visual field did not come up as high, and he lost his peripheral vision. We scheduled eye appointments, and as we looked at pictures of his eye on the computer, the ophthalmologist said, *"See that? You have a detached retina."* He scheduled an emergency surgery and told us we needed to be at the hospital within 20 minutes.

That night changed my perspectives on many things. I'll tell you now that things went well, and it looks like at the end of the two months his eye will be recovering, his sight will be back to normal, or almost normal. But as I waited for the surgery to be completed, thoughts ran through my mind, such as how important our sight is . . . how important my husband is to me . . . how quickly circumstances can change . . . how we go through life oblivious to how important we are to each other, except on rare and momentous occasions.

Being a wordsmith, I began exploring the meaning in the word *perspective* once we were home and in recovery. The center of the word has the same root as the word spectacles, the old-fashioned term for eyeglasses; or spectacular, or inspection, or suspect. All of the words have to do with sight.

Helen Keller said, "*The only thing worse than being blind is having sight but no vision.*" The vision that we gain when we are able to have perspective allows us to see things as they really are and have vision for how things really can be.

Having raised eight amazing human beings, I now can look back with a different and more mature perspective to times in my life when things were hectic, stressed, and chaotic . . . and those were on the better days, ha! The perspective of time and experience allows me to look back and be a lot kinder to parents going through that same season in their lives. I can smile with sympathetic compassion when I see a toddler having a tantrum in the grocery store. I can even see the person cutting me off in traffic and make a pretty good attempt to find a "righteous reason" for her behavior. Maybe her spouse didn't kiss her goodbye that morning. Maybe she's rushing to the hospital because she wants to see her loved one. Maybe she just got some terrible, life-altering news. Perspective changes how we see things, and time changes our perspective.

A word that sounds very similar to *perspective* is *perception*. Their meanings are somewhat related but definitely not the same. Where perspective involves vision, perception also mainly involves the mind and other senses. Perspective can change based on our vantage point, whether that is physical or point in time. Perception can be altered based on our intuition, and it can be the key to understanding the circumstances around us more fully. When my husband came out of the surgery, he had no depth perception in his right eye. In fact, his vision completely disappeared in his right eye. Now he can perceive variations in light and dark and slight color differentiations. He was able to see a slight difference when turning his eyes toward the shutters. But his vision will not be restored until greater recovery has taken place. At that point he will have new perspectives, based on his improved perceptions.

What do we do when we are struggling with our vision? If it's our physical sight, we see an ophthalmologist. But what about our view of ourselves? How do we look at our children differently when they are driving us crazy? What about the way we view events in our past or present? How about our vision for our future? How can we change our view of the people around us? How can we learn to view possibilities in a new way? How can we really SEE the ones we care about and treasure our time with them?

When we get depressed, or overwhelmed, discouraged; when we start feeling lost or purposeless; or we feel like we are in a rut so deep we cannot escape, what is really happening is that our perception is skewed and we need to create or adopt a new perspective. Someone once said that the only difference between a rut and a grave is the dimensions. I've also heard that a rut is a grave with the ends knocked out. Either way, that's not a good or happy place to be. That's not where we find joy, and it doesn't help us to stay on purpose.

I'm going to provide you with some very simple things you can do to help yourself get out of a rut. Most of them require no money, and they all are so easy that it doesn't take much effort. When you are depressed, making ANY effort is sometimes too much. Making simple changes empowers you to begin building again, this time with greater courage and a broader perspective. Once those shift, your perception will increase, and you will begin once more to feel guided in your decisions and your actions.

Here's your assignment. Read my list and jot down whatever speaks to you. You can keep it handy for whenever your perspective is a bit twisted and you need an adjustment.

1. Find an unusual person to make your friend.

2. Visit unusual places (once we read about a mailbox museum, and I decided that was just the ticket to get me out of my slump. Unfortunately, we drove for a couple of hours and never found the museum, but fortunately, the pleasant drive and fun conversation got me out of the slump!). So find an unusual place and give it a try. Ghost towns, historic sites, quirky festivals, rock hunting, picnics . . . you come up with more.

3. Adopt an unusual hobby. Some people paint pottery, or take cooking classes, or make cheese, or go visit people in rest homes and sing to them.

4. Wear something unusual. Bright colors can brighten your day.

5. Buy a magazine you've never bought before.

6. Try a food you've never tried before. You can cook it yourself, or you can try it in a restaurant. I was not terribly excited to order the quinoa/ kale salad but it turned out to be absolutely delicious!

7. Go to bed an hour earlier and wake up naturally without an alarm.

8. Take a new route home. Try the side streets and appreciate the landscaping and lawn decor.

9. Use green or purple or turquoise ink for informal notes to friends. Maybe hot pink?

10. Take a walk with someone instead of watching TV.

11. Give a "difficult person" in your life a sincere compliment. For example: "You have such lovely teeth" or "I love your smile" or "I appreciate your integrity."

12. Look through a mail order catalog and send yourself a present.

13. Leave for work ten minutes early and let people cut in front of you in traffic.

14. Drop a social activity you really don't care for.

15. Get a double-dip ice cream cone.

16. Change your toothpaste brand or flavor.

17. Send a silly card to someone.

18. Browse in a bookstore.

19. Go to a thrift store and pick out an interesting title to read, a cute used outfit to wear, or some random fun thing to decorate with.

20. Buy yourself a new wallet.

21. Keep the news off for seven days (I promise the world will continue on without you knowing the latest news).

22. Attend church services at a different church or synagogue or temple.

23. Change parking places.

24. Sleep on the other side of the bed.

25. Write a thank-you letter.

26. Get a therapeutic massage. You are worth it!

27. Do something you have always wanted to do but have postponed.

28. Is there a place you have always wanted to visit, but you haven't gone there? Begin researching the place and plan an itinerary. If it's a foreign country, you can write to their consulate, and sometimes they will send you pictures and posters and cool free things to help you plan your trip.

29. Join a health club.

30. Plan a month of recipes that are healthy and tasty. Then cook and freeze your premeasured meals.

31. Redecorate.

32. Put a funny cartoon on someone's desk.

33. Eliminate sugar from your diet for seven days.

34. Rearrange the furniture.

35. Watch a hilarious movie and let yourself laugh.

36. Put the toilet paper roll so it rolls the other way.

37. Try something totally different for breakfast; a new cereal or a unique hot dish.

38. Eat breakfast for dinner.

39. Run up and down the stairs three times.

40. Drop a "lucky" dollar bill on the sidewalk and make someone's day.

41. Rent a foreign film with subtitles from the library.

42. Tell a joke.

43. Give someone a verbal or physical pat on the back.

44. Go to a pet store.

45. Buy a box of crayons and a coloring book at the dollar store. Then color to relieve stress. That's especially fun with grandkids, but buy them their own crayons and books.

46. Try an exotic herbal tea.

47. Have a footbath.

48. Play "tourist" for a day in your home town.

49. Buy yourself an ant farm or some other toy you always wanted but never got as a child.

50. Buy a blank book and write down your thoughts.

51. Compose a poem.

52. Take a bath or shower by candlelight.

53. Take some flowers to a nursing home or a friend in need.

54. Clean your car inside and out.

55. Write down ten things you are grateful for.

56. Make a list of all the positive things about your friend or spouse.

57. Say a prayer.

58. Take a nap.

59. Take some time to dream about what you want and write it down.

60. Make dinner as a surprise and deliver it to someone who has need of extra help or love.

Will you let me know what you tried and what happened when you did? I'd love to hear from you. You can also send me a comment on my website.

Heritage James said, "*When you focus all your attention on what is seen, your eyes will be blinded to what is real. You must see the invisible, dream the impossible, and believe the unfathomable.*"

Chapter 8: Principles vs Policies

Time and time again, my clients have come to me with the same dilemma: you want to make wise decisions, and yet you want to be obedient to law. What do you do when the two seem to be in conflict? This chapter will give you some valuable tools to help you accomplish just that. Your successful implementation of the tools I give you will be based on your understanding of divine law and how it relates to principles vs. policies. Once you get those relationships clear in your mind and heart, making decisions and planning your goals will become MUCH easier. I promise!

First and foremost, everything–and I mean everything!–operates according to divine law. You can see it in everything from the cycles in the seasons to the order in the planets and their rotations. You can see it in the microscopic functions of blood cells and organs in your body. You can see it in the calculations that are involved in space travel and in surgery. Perhaps most importantly, you can see it in what you choose to do and how it affects you. Over time, as you observe the results of your actions, you can get better and better at knowing the laws and aligning with them to achieve your desired results.

This concept is so vital that it is one of the core principles in my coaching program. When we make the decisions and visualize what we want in our lives and then take the time and effort to understand and implement the laws by which those results come about, we can literally create the person we want to become and the experiences we want to have. We can also call into existence things we desire. All of these are just as certain as the laws they are founded upon. The one unknown is the amount of time it will take for some of those results and experiences and possessions to happen.

This has profound implications for each of us. Not only does it take away our excuses or ability to be a victim, but it also empowers us to literally achieve our dreams.

For many of us, when we hear the word *law*, we immediately think about the laws that govern our cities, communities, and nation. We think about "breaking the law" when we go over the speed limit, or we don't support a law that is on the books.

Here's the difference: God's laws are based upon principles. Man's laws are based on policies. Principles do not change. Policies can change as often as those in charge of policies desire to make changes. This creates a challenge: how can I be obedient to law when the laws change every time a new leader is voted into place?

The answer lies in realizing that when we correctly choose to be obedient to law, we are being obedient to the principles by which divine law operates. We are not beholden to the whimsical and ever-changing policies that man creates in order to govern or attain control.

Here's a way to make every decision work according to divine law. You first need to determine if the question is based on policies or on principles. That can be difficult at first, but it gets easier with practice. Ask yourself this question: Did a human being or a governing body make these policies? Can I figure out what divine laws are in place here and make a decision based upon my desired outcome? according to divine law?

Another important aspect of this concept to understand is that divine laws have counterfeits, so it can be confusing until we have figured that out. As a few examples: the counterfeit to faith is fear. So if we misinterpret the true law, we might say we are afraid we are making the wrong decision, and we want to wait before we take action. The counterfeit to action is paralysis. The counterfeit to respect is exploitation. If a couple is working on their marriage and they want to truly develop a divine and loving relationship, they need to be very aware of respecting each other versus exploiting each other for selfish reasons.

It's worth your time to explore these concepts! Be aware that you may think you are acting in accordance with divine law, but you need to be sure it's not a counterfeit to true law.

The reality is we can create our desired outcome, as we envision it, as long as we follow the divine laws in place. These are the same laws by which ALL creation takes place.

Disney introduced a wonderful musical interpretation of this concept in Pinocchio, with the song: "When You Wish upon a Star." Listen to these marvelous words:

When You Wish Upon a Star

When a star is born
They possess a gift or two
One of them is this:
They have the power to make a wish come true
When you wish upon a star
Makes no difference who you are
Anything your heart desires will come to you
If your heart is in your dream
No request is too extreme
When you wish upon a star
As dreamers do
Fate is kind
She brings to those who love
The sweet fulfillment of their secret longing
Like a bolt out of the blue
Fate steps in and sees you through
When you wish upon a star
Your dreams come true
When you wish upon a star
Makes no difference who you are
Anything your heart desires will come to you

If I had the ability (and since this is my book I'm claiming that right!), I would change one word in the song. I would change the word *fate* to the word *faith*. There is an element to faith, and to fervent prayer, that creates outcomes far more powerful and far-reaching than fate can do . . . that is, if you believe in fate.

In a previous chapter, I quoted Boyd K. Packer on faith. His words bear repeating:

There are two kinds of faith. One of them functions ordinarily in the life of every soul. It is the kind of faith born by experience; it gives us certainty that a new day will dawn, that spring will come, that growth will take place. It is the kind of faith that relates us with confidence to that which is scheduled to happen.

There is another kind of faith, rare indeed. This is the kind of faith that causes things to happen. It is the kind of faith that is worthy and prepared and unyielding, and it calls forth things that otherwise would not be. It is the kind of faith that moves people. It is the kind of faith that sometimes moves things. . . . It comes by gradual growth. It is a marvelous, even a transcendent, power, a power as real and as invisible as electricity. Directed and channeled, it has great effect.

When you pray, with full intent in your heart, I believe God hears you. In my Bible dictionary I find this powerful element in the definition of prayer:

Prayer is the act by which the will of the Father and the will of the child are brought into correspondence with each other. The object of prayer is not to change the will of God but to secure for ourselves and for others blessings that God is already willing to grant but that are made conditional on our asking for them. Blessings require some work or effort on our part before we can obtain them. Prayer is a form of work and is an appointed means for obtaining the highest of all blessings.

So...are you ready to do the work it takes to achieve your

dreams? I have met SO many people who want to help others. But first you have to learn to be successful yourself and then do the work to show you can. When you do that, people who are looking for answers will be drawn to what you can share with them. When we link our creative gifts as God's children with our efforts in accordance with His laws, we can learn and then apply the exact law or laws to help us achieve our desired results.

One of the most important elements in following the laws is making a decision. Decisions surround you and occupy a great deal of your attention. Even when you do nothing, you have made a decision to do nothing. But making a decision and then acting upon your decision will empower you to be of greater service, if that is what you desire to do. It will also empower you more fully to accomplish anything else you desire, according to law.

Sometimes (in fact often!) we are so anxious to choose the right choices, to do the right things, that we are stuck and can't decide ANYTHING. Dr. Seuss wrote about that in his story about the Zode. I love how he combines humor and hope with how to achieve your dreams.

The Zode in the Road
by Dr. Seuss

Did I ever tell you about the young Zode,
Who came to two signs at the fork in the road?
One said to Place One, and the other, Place Two.
So the Zode had to make up his mind what to do.

Well...the Zode scratched his head,
And his chin and his pants.
And he said to himself, "I'll be taking a chance
If I go to Place One. Now, that place may be hot!
And so, how do I know if I'll like it or not?
On the other hand though, I'll be sort of a fool
If I go to Place Two and find it too cool.
In that case I may catch a chill and turn blue!
So, maybe Place One is the best, not Place Two,
But then again, what if Place One is too high?
I may catch a terrible earache and die!
So Place Two may be best! On the other hand though...
What might happen to me if Place Two is too low?
I might get some very strange pain in my toe!
So Place One may be best," and he started to go.
Then he stopped, and he said, "On the other hand
though....
On the other hand...other hand...other hand though..."
And for 36 hours and a half that poor Zode
Made starts and made stops at the fork in the road.
Saying, "Don't take a chance. No! You may not be
right."
Then he got an idea that was wonderfully bright!
"Play safe!" cried the Zode. "I'll play safe. I'm no dunce!
I'll simply start out for both places at once!"
And that's how the Zode who would not take a chance
Got no place at all with a split in his pants.

The word *decision* has the same root as the word *scissors*, and it involves choosing what to cut. When we fail to decide, we decide to fail.

Once you make a decision, you can take action. And once you take action, you allow God to steer you in the best direction for you to go. You've probably heard that God does not steer a parked car. But once you move forward with faith in Him and His laws, you can achieve all that you desire.

Remember, every effort you give makes a difference. It is sometimes through accomplishing our goals and dreams that we inspire or help others to accomplish theirs.

Chapter 9: What's Stopping You?

A few years ago, my husband and I went down to Guatemala to visit my sister and her husband. They gave me a gift that I treasure: a lovely necklace and matching earrings. Then they told me the story of Creamos. The story made my gift even more precious.

For generations, hundreds of families, usually led by single moms, lived in the dumps in Guatemala They foraged for scraps of food, had no access to clean water or clothing, and had no chance for furthering their opportunities through education.

One day, a volunteer in the country thought of an idea to help them and to empower them to be able to provide for themselves and literally earn their way out of the dumps. The volunteer, Anna Hadingham, had some experience with creating jewelry out of recyclables. She showed the ladies how to cut thin, long, triangular strips from the glossy pages of discarded magazines, glue and roll them, and create amazingly beautiful beads. The beads were then strung together into lovely earrings, necklaces, and bracelets.

The ladies were exhilarated and motivated with this training! For the first time in many years, they could see hope and a pathway to achieving their dreams of going to school, being healthy, keeping their children safe, and moving on to a better way of life. Thus Creamos was formed.

Creamos offered safe and dignified income-generating opportunities for the mothers of the children, helping children break the cycle of poverty through education, life skills, and perseverance in the community surrounding the Guatemala City garbage dump. This amazing and amazingly successful program has now been in existence for nineteen years, disrupting the cycle of poverty within the community.

Sometimes we can become paralyzed with fear when we are faced with challenges that perplex us. We don't have experience with how to solve the challenge, and we feel stuck. As in the case with the Guatemalan families, that "stuck" can continue for generations. But—and here's the point of this chapter—you can find the solution. And the solution is somewhere in the vast accumulation of resources that surround you. So what's stopping you?

In the case of the Guatemalan ladies, the solution is in the thousands, even millions, of magazines that fill the dump. Their resources are unlimited and free! And they come from the very place that had caused them to be "stuck" for generations. All they needed was someone with an idea to solve the problem and teach them, and now their families benefit from her service.

I marvel at this story, all the more powerful because it is true and it has had such profound results. But it's not the only story like that:

In Cateura, Paraguay, indigent families discovered how to create instruments from trash. Favio Chavez founded an orchestra nearly thirteen years ago. Because none of the students could afford an instrument, Chavez asked Nicolas Gomez, a ganchero and a former carpenter at Cateura to help solve the challenge (a ganchero is a guy who uses a hook to dig through the garbage at the dump in search of anything he can use). Gomez worked tirelessly to create musical instruments with things he found in the landfill. After much trial and error, he created the pieces that now make up the Recycled Orchestra of Cateura. Among his clever inventions are a drum made with X-Rays as lining, a violin that uses a fork, and a bass made up of an old oil can. "*My life would be worthless without music,*" says one girl. A young man has a cello fashioned out of an oil can and old cooking tools.

A video clip, which introduced the world to the Recycled Orchestra of Cateura, quickly went viral. And now, kids from Cateura are flocking to join the orchestra. A ten-year-old girl who plays the violin, says that she looked up to some of the older girls in the ensemble and saw all the amazing opportunities they were having to travel well beyond Paraguay: "*I wanted to play because it seemed like they liked what they were playing,*" she says, "*and I wanted to visit other countries.*"

Money the orchestra has generated from its international touring has funded the building of new, safer homes for several members of the group and their families—and the orchestra's lead instrument maker, Nicolas Gomez.

Chavez says there's also been a bigger change. "*What we have achieved,*" he says, "*is that in the community, children are respected. And respect for the moment that they need to get an education. It's something sacred. Before, it wasn't like this. Before I gave music classes, the mom or dad would take the kid away by the hand because they had to go to work. Today, that's unthinkable, impossible for it to happen. And we've already achieved the most difficult thing, which is to change the community.*"

Chavez says that the kids playing in the Recycled Orchestra are creating something gorgeous out of nothing. "*To be a musician,*" he says, "*you have to be responsible, persistent, tenacious, conscientious and sensitive. Without these values, you can't be a musician. But music has such a great power that it can't be just of the musicians. Music can transform society.*"

"*People realize that we shouldn't throw away trash carelessly,*" says Chavez. "*Well, we shouldn't throw away people either.*"

Someone posted on Facebook about the fear they feel when they realize that they do not have enough money. She asked how to get past that fear. This was my response:

Your solution is only an idea + action away, and you can pray for divine inspiration helping you brainstorm. The reality is that money is merely a symbol. You always have all that you need. Sometimes you can sell things, sometimes you can create something, sometimes you can take on extra hours of work; . . . the list is endless. I say this having been in what I felt was the worst possible financial crisis I could have. Hold on to your faith and God will see you through with shelter, clothing, food, water, and love. Write a lot of possibilities and pray over your list before you sleep and ask for ideas to come to you. Be at peace and pray and ponder with great gratitude for how you have been cared for in the past.

Dr. Seuss wrote about that in his story *Oh! The Places You'll Go!* In his endearing style of humor with profound wisdom, Seuss starts this marvelous story with upbeat words of encouragement and confidence that the reader can go anywhere and achieve anything he or she desires.

Congratulations!
Today is your day.
You're off to Great Places!
You're off and away!
You have brains in your head.
You have feet in your shoes.
You can steer yourself
any direction you choose.
You're on your own. And you know what you know.
And YOU are the guy who'll decide where to go.
You'll look up and down streets. Look 'em over with care.
About some you will say, 'I don't choose to go there.'
With your head full of brains and your shoes full of feet,
you're too smart to go down any not-so-good street.

Then Dr. Seuss gets into the place where we can become stuck. We can become depressed and paralyzed in our efforts to move forward.

Wherever you fly, you'll be best of the best.
Wherever you go, you will top all the rest.
Except when you don't.
Because, sometimes, you won't.
I'm sorry to say so
but, sadly, it's true
that Bang-ups
and Hang-ups
can happen to you.
You can get all hung up
in a prickle-ly perch.
And your gang will fly on.
You'll be left in a Lurch.
You'll come down from the Lurch
with an unpleasant bump.
And the chances are, then,
that you'll be in a Slump.
And when you're in a Slump,
you're not in for much fun.
Un-slumping yourself
is not easily done.
You will come to a place where the streets are not marked.
Some windows are lighted. But mostly they're darked.
A place you could sprain both your elbow and chin!
Do you dare to stay out? Do you dare to go in?

How much can you lose? How much can you win?
And IF you go in, should you turn left or right...
or right-and-three-quarters? Or, maybe, not quite?
Or go around back and sneak in from behind?
Simple it's not, I'm afraid you will find,
for a mind-maker-upper to make up his mind.

If this describes you, you're not alone. Obviously, Dr. Seuss experienced feelings like this because his descriptions of the mindset we have when we are stuck is so profound.

You can get so confused
that you'll start in to race
down long wiggled roads at a break-necking pace
and grind on for miles cross weirdish wild space,
headed, I fear, toward a most useless place.
The Waiting Place...
...for people just waiting.
Waiting for a train to go
or a bus to come, or a plane to go
or the mail to come, or the rain to go
or the phone to ring, or the snow to snow
or the waiting around for a Yes or No
or waiting for their hair to grow.
Everyone is just waiting.
Waiting for the fish to bite
or waiting for the wind to fly a kite
or waiting around for Friday night
or waiting, perhaps, for their Uncle Jake

or a pot to boil, or a Better Break
or a string of pearls, or a pair of pants
or a wig with curls, or Another Chance.
Everyone is just waiting.
I'm afraid that some times
you'll play lonely games too.
Games you can't win
'cause you'll play against you.
All Alone!
Whether you like it or not,
Alone will be something
you'll be quite a lot.

If you can't tell, I really love the insights in Dr. Seuss's books. I'm not as fond of his illustrations, but that's just me. They are certainly original! And Dr. Seuss was a man who faced and transcended countless rejections and refusals before he finally, with persistence, achieved the results he wanted. The legacy he created with his brains, his art, and his persistence lives on in the lives of countless children today (and their parents).

On and on you will hike,
And I know you'll hike far
and face up to your problems
whatever they are.
You're off to Great Places!
Today is your day!
Your mountain is waiting.

So . . . get on your way!

If you are, or you have been, in a place where you didn't know the next step . . . if you feel stuck . . . if you are fearful . . . if you feel down, literally, in the dumps, . . . I hope this chapter has given you the fuel you need to use your brain and your inspiration to come up with the idea and action that will move you into hope, achievement, persistence, and prosperity. Remember, the Law of Polarity says that the low tides are followed by the high tides. The oceans ebb and flow. The sun rises and sets. Darkness is followed by light; winter is followed by spring. Remember, every effort you give makes a difference.

What's stopping you? Give yourself permission to think, to pray, to come up with ideas and inspiration. Give yourself the chance to fail and fall and try again! Give yourself the grace to know that you can create exactly the results you want by following the laws of success and the ideas that come to you. Never give up. Stay the course and keep at it, and in the end, you will be unstoppable!

Chapter 10: Every Precious Moment

While in the midst of raising our children, I remember one particular day amazingly well, considering that the two-year-old of whom I speak is now thirty years old.

We had eight children, but he was the youngest of three toddlers at the bottom of the eight. I was feeling a bit under the weather and overwhelmed with the mess that surrounded me. My two-year-old had brought a tuna sandwich into our bedroom. He had a messy diaper and I didn't want to change it. I kept hoping in the back of my mind that someone else, somewhere, would come and change it for me. Earlier this same son had brought a bowl of Rice Krispies into the bedroom. Fortunately he didn't have milk in the bowl. In getting these and other items out in the kitchen, he had spilled a jar of pickles onto the floor and walked through the pickle juice before spilling the Rice Krispies he had poured into the bowl and onto the pickle juice.

I hadn't slept well the night before, and although I'm typically an early riser, I was hoping for a few minutes in bed before I had to face the day. But my little Nathaniel had different ideas. He climbed onto the bed with his pickle-juice, Rice Krispie–sticky feet, holding his dripping tuna sandwich, stinking with his messy diaper, and he began to jump enthusiastically on my clean bedcovers.

As I look back now, I can laugh and realize my little boy was probably trying to cheer me up by jumping on the bed, and he had been hungry with a mommy who wasn't getting him breakfast so he was happily fending for himself. But in my haze of exhaustion I couldn't see it then, and I was in tears. My mind was thinking *"I'll never ever be able to clean this and him up." And probably something along the line of, "and I will never be able to be happy again."*

They say tragedy plus time equals humor, and now I can chuckle about that visual from so many years ago. But when one of my daughters or my sons tells me about their eighteen-month-old throwing his chocolate oatmeal onto himself, the wall, the floor and his siblings, my mind goes back to those days. They weren't easy. They weren't even fun a lot of the time. But they were precious.

Of course it's a wise practice to look ahead, to anticipate, to plan for the future. But true joy can only be found in the present moment, when we fully embrace the season of our lives we are living in, and we can feel gratitude for our current circumstances and situations, even when they are very challenging.

Our current circumstances may be financial stress or uncertainty, health issues, relationship issues, raising family issues, stress or worry, or fear of unknown. The reality is that very little we worry about ever happens. When we can get into a head space where we can learn to savor the moments that stretch us but fulfill us, we are living our purpose and experiencing joy in a big way.

A report in the *Guardian* caught my eye. Bronnie Ware, an Australian nurse who spent several years working in palliative care, cared for patients in the last 12 weeks of their lives. She recorded their dying epiphanies in a book called *The Top Five Regrets of the Dying*.

Ware writes of the phenomenal clarity of vision that people gain at the end of their lives, and how we might learn from their wisdom. "*When questioned about any regrets they had or anything they would do differently,*" she says, "*common themes surfaced again and again.*"

Here are the top five regrets of the dying, as witnessed by Ware:

I wish I'd had the courage to live a life true to myself, not the life others expected of me.

I wish I hadn't worked so hard.

I wish I'd had the courage to express my feelings.

I wish I had stayed in touch with my friends.

I wish that I had let myself be happier.

Ware wrote: "*This is a surprisingly common one. Many did not realize until the end that happiness is a choice. They had stayed stuck in old patterns and habits. The so-called 'comfort' of familiarity overflowed into their emotions, as well as their physical lives. Fear of change had them pretending to others, and to their selves, that they were content, when deep within, they longed to laugh properly and have silliness in their life again.*"

I hope you make note of these five regrets and make sure that you think about them in looking ahead for your life. I'm going to take each of these points and share some ideas about how to handle each of those in such a way that you don't arrive at the end of your life with unfulfilled dreams, full of regret.

Boyd K. Packer told of a time he visited an elderly widow. *"I was not [yet] married at the time and occasionally . . . I would go down and get her some lemon ice cream, and she appreciated it.*

One evening, she decided that she wanted to give me some counsel. She told me the story of her life. Marriage . . . to a wonderful [man], living together and beginning a family. . . .

Then she focused in on a Monday morning. A blue dreary wash day, gray and cloudy outside and in. Cross children, a little irritation, a poor meal, and finally an innocent remark by one, snapped up by the other, and soon husband and wife were speaking crossly and critically to one another.

As he left for work, she said, I just had to follow him to the gate. And call out one last biting and spiteful remark after him.

And then as the tears came, she told me of an accident that day . . . and he didn't return from work.

For 50 years, she sobbed, "I've regretted that the last words he ever heard from my lips was that one last biting spiteful remark."

In an instant, our lives can change. All that we assume will last forever as we go about our busy days does not stay constant, much as we wish it could. If we can create a patient perspective with ourselves and others, we will not regret thoughtless comments and moments of anger or frustration, because we will have learned how to deal with them BEFORE they cause pain to our loved ones, especially the little ones. Really, aren't we all little and vulnerable?

Bronnie Ware's first regret in her book:

I wish I'd had the courage to live a life true to myself, not the life others expected of me.

One of the greatest concerns people in their younger and middle-aged years has with this point is this: we don't know ourselves enough to know if we are true to ourselves or not. How can we figure it out? And how do we achieve a place of peace with ourselves, knowing we are living up to our own wishes for our life?

For now, you can take a survey of yourself, and keep track of what brings you joy, what qualities you and others notice in you that are significant to you. I am a firm believer in writing things down. So keep a journal where you can keep these records and refer back to them.

Once you have identified what brings you joy (whether in work, relationships, or play), begin to act on them. If we are talking about relaxation, think about the root word *lax*, which means "careless, negligent, loose or slack." Not exactly how I want to be. Now think of a word we also use and we sometimes confuse the two: Recreation. The root of "recreation" is create, or creation. To find true fulfillment and happiness, you have to allow your creative mind to find solutions.

And I'm not talking about the escapee-type things we fall back on when we're sick or stressed or need a change. No one is going to come to the end of their life regretting that they didn't finish that television series or jump out of an airplane. Ok, maybe the airplane, but honestly, there are more important things. So go for recreation, not relaxation.

I wish I hadn't worked so hard.

This one is simple but oh! so hard to implement. Find what you love to do and do that for your work. Why is it hard to implement? Because you're moving ahead in total faith when you do that. We can be so desperate for money that we sacrifice who we are and limit our goals to only working within the parameters that currently are our situation. Folks, if you don't feel good about where you are, take courage and begin to move into another direction that fills your heart with joy. You can keep working, but begin working toward your desired goal. You do NOT have to stay stuck in a livelihood you will regret on your deathbed. You CAN do this. I promise that over time you will be glad you did.

I wish I'd had the courage to express my feelings.

It's tough when we don't know how our feelings will be accepted, and we don't know if they are reciprocated. But if you don't ask, and you don't try, the answer is always no. And it you don't risk, you can never attain.

Risks
  by Leo F. Buscaglia

To laugh is to risk appearing a fool,
To weep is to risk appearing sentimental.
To reach out to another is to risk involvement,
To expose feelings is to risk exposing your true self.
To place your ideas and dreams before a crowd is to risk their loss.
To love is to risk not being loved in return,
To live is to risk dying,
To hope is to risk despair,
To try is to risk failure.
But risks must be taken because the greatest hazard in life is to risk nothing.
The person who risks nothing, does nothing, has nothing, is nothing.
He may avoid suffering and sorrow,
But he cannot learn, feel, change, grow or live.
Chained by his servitude he is a slave who has forfeited all freedom.
Only a person who risks is free."

I wish I had stayed in touch with my friends.

Dinah Maria Mulock Craik said this, in *A Life for a Life*:
  "*Oh, the comfort — the inexpressible comfort of feeling safe with a person — having neither to weigh thoughts nor measure*

words, but pouring them all right out, just as they are, chaff and grain together; certain that a faithful hand will take and sift them, keep what is worth keeping, and then with the breath of kindness blow the rest away."

I wish that I had let myself be happier

In the past few weeks I have learned of two friends dying very young, one in his forties and one at the age of 52. These were the kind of people who were able to pour a lifetime of love and service and joy into their shorter lifespans. But when you look around at your class reunion and realize how many have already gone on before, time becomes infinitely more valuable as you look ahead to how many years you potentially have in front of you. What have you done with your time? And more importantly, what are you going to do with the time you have left?

Benjamin Franklin said, *"Dost thou love life?*

Then do not squander time, for that is the stuff life is made of."

How do you live a life with no regrets? I think small regrets are inevitable, because we learn by experience. But overall, think about all the majesty that surrounds you: this amazing planet, with its oceans, sky, animals, mountains, trees, and wonderful, miraculous souls that fill it. Every day we can gaze in wonder at a completely unique sunrise, and then applaud God's artistry again at night when the sun sets. What a gift, to have a life! And what an even greater gift to have the miracles that are our bodies, so that we can experience all the incredible feelings of joy and gratitude and love and wonder!

If you're not happy (and I'm talking about long-term unhappiness), you need help getting your head and your health back to a place where you can be whole again. But if you're caught up in the pressures and stresses of a life that is making you even more pressured and stressed, it's time to take a step back and REALLY THINK about what you want.

What do you want to make sure you do before you leave this plane of existence? What do you want to leave as a legacy, to gift to others who follow? Who do you want to learn with, and grow with, and experience life and love with?

Don't be like the dour old Scotsman who was greeting guests at his wife's wake. "*Fergus,*" said his friends, "*yer wife were a treasure. Ye must've loved her mightily.*" "*Aye,*" Fergus said, "*an' I nearly told her so once.*"

Years ago, Erma Bombeck wrote a beautiful reminder of enjoying the present moment. I cried when I read it the first time, and I hope I can get through it now as I share it with you. It's a profound reminder to cherish these fleeting moments we have with our loved ones, especially our littles.

WET OATMEAL KISSES
Erma Bombeck

The baby is teething. The children are fighting. Your husband just called and said, "Eat dinner without me." One of these days you'll explode and shout to the kids, "Why don't you grow up and act your age?" And they will.

Or, "You guys get outside and find yourselves something to do. And don't slam the door!" And they don't. You'll straighten their bedrooms all neat and tidy, toys displayed on the shelf, hangers in the closet, animals caged. You'll yell, "Now I want it to stay this way!" And it will.

You will prepare a perfect dinner with a salad that hasn't had all the olives picked out and a cake with no finger traces in the icing and you'll say, "Now THIS is a meal for company." And you will eat it alone.

You'll say, "I want complete privacy on the phone. No dancing around, no pantomimes, no demolition crews. Silence! Do you hear?" and you'll have it. No more plastic tablecloths stained with spaghetti, no more anxious nights under a vaporizer tent, no more dandelion bouquets, no more iron-on patches, wet, knotted shoestrings, tight boots, missing mittens, or ponytails falling out.

Imagine, a lipstick with a point, no babysitter, washing clothes only once a week, no parent meetings, carpools, Christmas presents out of toothpicks and paste.

No more wet oatmeal kisses.

No more tooth fairy, giggles in the dark, or knees to heal.

Only a voice crying, "Why don't you grow up?" and the silence echoing,

"I did."

Let love and light and laughter be your legacy to leave the world. There is only one YOU, with YOUR unique dreams, talents, goals, and passion. Be a light to everyone around you. Let your light shine on broken hearts and broken dreams, especially your own. Be kind to yourself when you mess up, and keep going. We're all learning, and we all make mistakes. Each time you can do and be a little better. You can do and be anything you want to be.

Chapter 11: When Others Don't Believe in You

What do you do when you have dreams and goals and no one (especially those you trust and look up to) supports you or believes in you? And as a corollary to that: How do you develop the courage to move forward with goals when everyone seems to doubt you.

It's a tough question. Even when you have had a near-perfect childhood, and we have given life and achievement and preparation and effort our best shot, it seems like there are those who tear you down; who want to let you know in advance that there's no way in heaven you can accomplish your wild, crazy, hare-brained plans. The worst of it is that these are usually the people who "love" you and support you as family and dearest friends. What gives with that scenario? Shouldn't they be all excited about your creative vision, your goals and dreams? And if they aren't, why aren't they?

Before I start in on why that happens and how to deal with it, I'm going to ask you a few questions: why do you feel a need for others to believe in you? Allow yourself to ponder that as you make the choices you'll be making. Are you thinking to spread the blame if you fail? Is your plan incomplete and you want to include others in executing the plan, so you need their expertise and input? Is your ego demanding that others fall in line with what you envision? Are you allowing others the opportunity to voice their opinion and taking it for whatever it's worth? Have you grown up with the philosophy that if others don't respond enthusiastically to your ideas, your ideas aren't valuable or realistic?

If you can separate your ego from the answers to all of these questions and then make the decision to move forward and believe in yourself, with or without their support, you're on the right track.

Goethe said this: "*If you treat an individual as he is, he will remain how he is. But if you treat him as if he were what he ought to be and could be, he will become what he ought to be and could be.*"

While we are looking into the lives of a number of people who have thumbed their noses at what other people thought and have gone on to achieve their dreams anyway, ask yourself: Am I treating myself as if I am what I ought to be and could be? Or am I hoping to get that validation from outside myself?

Jesus said, "*Love thy neighbor as thyself.*" In order to do that, you have to be able to love yourself. And the upshot of that is: you have to be able to believe in yourself, that you are worthy of love and that you deserve to accomplish what you desire to accomplish (as long as you are willing to put in the effort and do what it takes).

History is FULL of people who dealt with massive resistance in trying to accomplish their dreams. In fact, it seems to be a requirement in most cases. Let's look at a few of the most famous ones:

I've always been inspired by Thomas Edison, who invented the light bulb, of course, and also moving pictures (what would we do without light? without movies?). Edison held nearly 1,100 patents and was the twentieth century's most prolific inventor. His life wasn't easy. He did not do well in elementary school. He was hyperactive and prone to distraction, so his mother pulled him out and taught him at home. But Edison's persistence paid off.

Here are some of his most inspiring quotes:

I have not failed. I've just found 10,000 ways that won't work.

Our greatest weakness lies in giving up. The most certain way to succeed is always to try just one more time.

Opportunity is missed by most people because it is dressed in overalls and looks like work.

Many times, those who criticize your plan are experts in their field. They may not have a clear vision of what you are wanting to accomplish. Here are some past solemn declarations that experts have made:

The Beatles were rejected by record label after record label. One notable response was "guitar groups are on the way out" and "*The Beatles have no future in show business.*"

"*The cinema is little more than a fad. It's canned drama. What audiences really want to see is flesh and blood on the stage.*" — Charlie Chaplin, actor, producer, director, and studio founder, 1916.

Barbara Streisand's mother said she'd never be a singer because her voice wasn't good enough and she'd never be pretty enough to be an actress.

"*The Americans have need of the telephone, but we do not. We have plenty of messenger boys.*" — Sir William Preece, Chief Engineer, British Post Office, 1878.

A modeling agency told Marilyn Monroe: "*You better get secretarial work or get married.*"

"*[Television] won't be able to hold on to any market it captures after the first six months. People will soon get tired of staring at a plywood box every night.*" — Darryl Zanuck, movie producer, 20th Century Fox, 1946.

Henry Morton, the president of the Stevens Institute of Technology, commented about Thomas Edison's light bulb: "*Everyone acquainted with the subject will recognize it as a conspicuous failure.*" Thomas Edison tried over 10,000 times to create the light bulb.

In a famous rejection letter, Rudyard Kipling was told by the San Francisco Examiner: "*I'm sorry, Mr. Kipling, but you just don't know how to use the English language.*"

Henry Ford was told that "*the horse is here to stay but the automobile is only a novelty, a fad.*"

Colonel Sanders began selling his famous "secret recipe" for his delectable fried chicken at the age of 65, after a lifetime of trying and failing at countless endeavors. If you want to gain the confidence to try, read about the Colonel's persistence.

J. K. Rowling received a letter from a publisher that claimed, "*Children just aren't interested in witches and wizards anymore.*" Rowling said, after living a very difficult life as a single mom, "*Happiness can be found, even in the darkest of times, if one only remembers to turn on the light. Whether you come back by page or by the big screen, Hogwarts will always be there to welcome you home. It is our choices . . . that show what we truly are, far more than our abilities.*" When Rowling signed up for welfare benefits, she described her economic status as being "*poor as it is possible to be in modern Britain, without being homeless.*"

There are countless types of people on this planet, and chances are, none of them are exactly like you. So how would they know what is your best option? Or what dream is going to work out for you or not? For sure, it won't work for them, because they are not exactly like you (even if they feel they know you really well), they can't see into your heart or know how much effort and vision you have already put into accomplishing this dream or goal you have.

If you have a clear vision of what you want to accomplish, get going on it, and don't let anything stop you.

"*How, sir, would you make a ship sail against the wind and currents by lighting a bonfire under her deck? I pray you, excuse me, I have not the time to listen to such nonsense.*" — Napoleon Bonaparte, when told of Robert Fulton's steamboat.

"*When the Paris Exhibition [of 1878] closes, electric light will close with it and no more will be heard of it.*" — Oxford professor Erasmus Wilson.

Van Gogh put up with not only verbal criticism but also complete shunning. He was unsuccessful in trying to sell his art.

Winston Churchill's father said that Winston was "*unfit for a career in law or politics.*"

So, when you add these past twenty examples, I think I've established that YOU can achieve YOUR goals, and act upon your ideas, regardless of what everyone is telling you that you can't do.

Why would the very people you love and trust and believe in try to squelch your dream?

Ironically, it's usually because they love you and care for you, and they want to see you happy and successful. But they want to spare you the pain of failure. Maybe they tried a similar venture into the unknown and it caused them pain, or they failed. Maybe they see the risk as too great. Maybe they can see that in choosing to follow after this dream you are neglecting major responsibilities. For example, if you have a spouse and family or others who will be affected by your choice, it's a good idea to involve them in the decision. If someone is investing financially in your goal, they have a right to be involved in the decision. If you fail and you fall back on someone else for support, that person should be involved in your decision. Think it through carefully, and think about what success or failure on your part might mean for someone else that is emotionally or financially invested in you.

Thomas Paine said, "*That which we obtain too easily, we esteem too lightly.*"

If you need a little more on this topic, check out Chapter

9: "What's Stopping You?" You can see that, to paraphrase what Thomas Paine said, if success comes too quickly or easily we may not fully appreciate what we have. Or we may not give it the true value it has created for us.

You can know that it's NOT going to be all roses and clover, and you need to be prepared for the walls and barriers and barricades you'll be facing if you want to live a life you dream of. I know where you're coming from. I've faced my share of Goliaths, trying to figure out where to aim my sling-shot. Or, in the case of family, where to place my trust and confidence with their input. Sometimes it's helpful, even when it hurts.

Sometimes—and this is a big one—they have watched you in the past and they have seen you start something ill prepared, and you have not carried your vision to completion. So if you are asking others to believe in you but you haven't shown them that they can believe you, you may want to make some changes in consistent follow through before you can hope for support.

Here are some key questions to ask yourself:

How important is this idea?

How much have your explored your idea?

What will it take to make the idea happen?

What are the possible obstacles you might face?

Can you be persistent?

Can you be consistent?

How strong is your belief in yourself?

How strong is your belief in your idea?

Are you committed to taking this all the way?

What could stop you from pursuing your goal?

Is it strong enough to keep going, even when you have only yourself to sustain the enthusiasm?

Once you've gotten clear on what you want to do, get going and make it happen.

The reality is that your life is YOUR life. You can change it by changing your thinking and then changing your actions. You have the ability to look at something and decide if it looks like a good choice or a poor one; if it looks like too much of a risk or if you are willing to throw everything you have into it to make it successful. If you have a vision, and you do all the foundation planning, and thinking, and researching, and prove to yourself that it's a good vision, with clear possibility, then ask God. He believes in you when no others do. But don't let Him down. And don't let yourself down. Do the work . . . all the legwork, to give yourself success. And be consistent and persistent until you do.

You are never too old to achieve your dream, and you are never too young to begin your dream. The worst place to be is having your dream and doing nothing about it. Moving slowly in the wrong direction is better than standing still. At least if you are moving you can get feedback from your failures and change your direction and momentum.

And here's the bottom line: There's only one person who HAS to believe in you, and that's you yourself.

Chapter 12: Great . . . and Not So Great . . . Expectations

One of my clients contacted me in despair. In decades of marriage, she had never felt love from her mother-in-law. In fact, it was just the opposite. She could almost feel the steam coming out of her mother-in-law's ears when she visited. My client felt that her mother-in-law expected her to be present at family activities, but she felt very unwelcome. It made it a chore to be there, and she had nightmares about upcoming re-unions and get-togethers.

If you are experiencing similar feelings toward family that becomes family when you marry, and you just can't quite see your way to thinking of them with anything but dread, this chapter is for you. And while your feelings may not change, you'll be able to get yourself into a better headspace about how to make it all work in your life and for you.

We spend the first two to three or more decades of our lives becoming who we are. Sometimes, especially in our teens and twenties, we begin thinking more seriously about long-lasting committed relationships . . . marriage. When we find the person who awakens a deep desire to spend our life with that person, we have all kinds of great expectations about how blissful life will be once we have vowed to love each other and forsake all others.

Then reality hits like a bolt of lightning.

Sometimes this happens in the planning stages for the wedding, and sometimes we can make it through until AFTER the wedding, but inevitably we will find ourselves at odds with the WEIRD way the "other" family interacts, or the way they talk, or the way they celebrate, or their strange traditions. It's the kind of thing ANYONE would notice, right? Their jokes are strange, their stories aren't amusing, you can't eat their food, and the list goes on. They are just so different. And everyone with eyes to see would notice that.

Not really. The reality is they are not you. And you really don't want them to be. Marriage would be pretty boring if you merged families as easily as a zipper pulls two sides together. Zipping a zipper might be less stressful, but you know how hard it can be to get a zipper to work once a zipper pull gets caught or the teeth on a zipper are bent.

Here's the deal: You come into a relationship with "great expectations" of how magical that relationship will be, ongoing. Brene Brown uses the very descriptive term of "the story we tell ourselves" about what is happening. We are falling in love, and our loved one is falling in love with us, but we have decades of living and growing and learning WITHOUT each other to mesh into a committed and ongoing state of happiness.

Robert Jordan said, "*He was swimming in a sea of other people's expectations. Men had drowned in seas like that.*"

By the way, the happiness will NOT be fixed and will not come by expecting your spouse to become like you, or to understand you perfectly, or to connect with you in ways that you expect. You're going to have to do some pretty serious and committed detective work to learn what each other means, what your love languages are, what is important to each other and why.

One spouse is absolutely enraptured with watching sports on TV. The other could care less. One spouse is a total techie, a nerd who loves to figure out code and write computer programs. The other is interested in how to teach the children to be kind to each other, or how to garden, or how to decorate or cook. One spouse is eager to work out every day. For the other, a walk in the park is the best exercise. Men and women often find that language itself is a barrier. We both speak the same language, but the words we use don't mean the same things to us as they do to our spouse.

It's all based on our expectations.

So what is the story we tell ourselves? We might have the expectation that a great mother-in-law speaks in a certain way, looks a certain way, welcomes us in a certain way. That's our story of what a good mother-in-law should be. However, unbeknownst to US, she has HER story of what a great daughter-in-law should be! And heaven help the woman who marries her perfect son, because there is no way anyone deserves as wonderful a man as he is. Same goes for the perfect daughter . . . no man can quite measure up to the perfection in a girl that she has raised and adored from the moment she was born. I'm using mothers-in-law as the example here, but fathers-in-law fit into the same picture with our "great expectations."

We have the ideal in our head, and we marry the one who most closely represents that ideal. But the story we are telling ourselves embellishes the ideal during that courtship phase when we are dating and there are hormones and attraction and kisses and desires . . . and the story we tell ourselves blissfully glides over the small sticky little issues that give a hint that we are different, after all, in our expectations.

Then we deal with the dissimilar reality of every day, that has been different for decades.

By the way, this doesn't disappear when you have been married a long time. You will find yourself constantly learning new details about each other as you are married, even after many years of marriage. You will discover how differently your spouse reacts to stress, or sickness, or disappointments, even successes. The effort to bring your love into a unifying connection is a constant and never-ending labor that requires each of us to let go of ego, let go of our great expectations, and be open and forgiving with each other and the stories we tell ourselves.

When our spouse disciplines the kids in a way that doesn't fit our expectations, we have to figure out how to work that out without coming to verbal blows with one another. We have to examine where we each come from, with our previous history and experiences, and create new union by zipping those two distinct backgrounds into one that is a hybrid of the two, and much more powerful and meaningful.

It might seem daunting to try to make that happen, and many times the effort is so exhausting that spouses give up or establish a "neutral zone" when conflict heats up to create on-going contention.

In this chapter, I'm going to give you a few ideas how to mitigate the conflict and the emotional chaos it creates. I'm also going to share with you some ways to overcome animosity toward your "in-law" family.

First of all, if at all possible BEFORE the wedding, study together about how marriage will be, and talk (and write down!) your expectations as clearly as you can. You can study and talk about your intimate expectations. You can talk about work, and finances, and education, and having a family or travel or other plans and goals you have. If you have gotten past that point and you're already married and in conflict, you can create a relaxed environment (translate that to a date) where you can do the same thing.

If she's a night owl and he's an early bird, that will all come into play too. You can't tell yourself the story that "*if he really loved me, he'd make the effort to stay up late with me.*" And your spouse can't tell himself the story that "*she should get up at the crack of dawn and go work out with me.*"

Give and take should not become a tug of war, and it should not have a winner and a loser. Over time, in a safe setting, each of you can assess what is most important and figure out what works for you both in the best way.

Your ego is not your amigo. Be willing to hear each other out. And it's especially helpful, when you feel emotions rising and getting more heated, to say to your spouse: "*The story I'm telling myself is...*" and finish expressing what your past history is dredging up for you. Let your spouse listen and you listen too. Make it safe to do that. It's tough, sometimes, to be honest and realize that your way is NOT the only way. It's just different.

One woman who had been married many years and had a number of children with her husband gave up, and they divorced. She confided in me later that she wished she had been more flexible and learned better how to work through things with him. She felt she had been too quick to judge his motives and too slow to accept her own role in elevating the emotional conflict and stress.

What about getting along with the in-laws? Remember, they have their own expectations of you how should be. And there's no way in the world you're going to fit that list 100%. No way!

So let them have whatever their list is! You don't need to know what's on their list. But you can say in your heart, "*The story that I'm telling myself is that a good mother-in-law has these qualities. But my mother-in-law has her own list of qualities that she thinks a good mother-in-law should have. And she also has her own list of qualities that a good daughter- or son-in-law should have. She is entitled to have her list, her own great expectations.*"

If the story you are telling yourself is that you cannot measure up to her expectations, that's just fine. You can just measure up to your own expectations. And allow her the grace to measure up to her own expectations.

One of my clients showed me a wedding invitation her future daughter-in-law had designed. My client was frustrated and angry as she pointed out all the errors and bad design features in the invitation. "*See the date is hardly visible, and the font she chose looks terrible! I can't stand the picture.*" I noted that there is more than one way to do a creative endeavor in the "right" way, and the wedding invitation is an area that she really doesn't have to own as her responsibility. So what if it's not a perfect invitation? So what if it doesn't fit the mother-in-law's standard? It's the bride and groom's prerogative to design their own invitation, unless the parents are paying for the invitation and they all agreed on the stewardship for the invitation's design beforehand.

Lisa Kleypas said, "*You are your own worst enemy. If you can learn to stop expecting impossible perfection, in yourself and others, you may find the happiness that has always eluded you.*"

Getting to the bottom of conflict is easier if you can identify the principles involved. It becomes safer to discover the principles when you allow each other to figure out, and express, the stories you are telling to yourselves. For example, if one spouse likes pitching a tent and sleeping under the stars, and the other prefers "glamping" in a hotel and going out to dinner. "*The story I'm telling myself is based on how my family went camping when I was a child, and we would really connect singing around the campfire. Would you be open to trying that with me? I'd like to see if I can create that kind of happy mem-*

ory for you." And then the other spouse has to let go of ego to try new experiences and be open to changing minds.

For every example I give of conflict, there are thousands of other iterations in which we can hurt and offend and judge one another. But the opportunity is there to love and understand, to be patient in learning from each other. One of my clients has found that she and her husband do best when they save any and all conflict to discuss in a more rational, less emotional way once a week in a family council. This is a great tool for making the "zipper" merge more smoothly. Sometimes, the issue that created emotional reaction disappears by the time family council is on the schedule, and other times more instances occur to reinforce the issue that is causing conflict. When that happens, it's easier to explain the disconnect in a way that both can understand and rearrange how to handle the issue.

To truly make a marriage union work, we have to trust each other's hearts. It is seldom that two people marry and one or both of them is deliberately trying to hurt or harm the other. If that is happening, get out and get out quickly. There are much worse things than divorce. Enlist the help of those you can trust and get away and be safe.

But when simple disagreements happen because of your disparate upbringings and backgrounds—and they inevitably will—establish a system to work through the conflict and create unity. There is nothing more satisfying than creating and developing a joyful, meaningful bond with one another that only enriches you both through the years.

So let's summarize the main tips and techniques you can

employ to get that zipper moving up smoothly, bringing the two of you together.

- Recognize from the outset that you are blending two completely different lives, with completely different experiences and backgrounds, including family traditions and dynamics.
- Recognize that there is no "one right way." Everyone can contribute ideas to make what is, better.
- Identify and share *"the story I am telling myself"* when you are stressed or experiencing conflict and mounting negative emotions. Learn to recognize what your expectations are, even when they are subconscious expectations for your spouse to fit your ideal. And if you are the spouse who is listening to the other's story, listen to understand, with great compassion and forgiveness. You are both learning.
- Listen with empathy and without ego. Your ego is not your amigo.
- Create a safe time and place, such as a family council, where you can share your concerns and the issues that are really important to you to see if you can combine ideas to create something that works for both of you.
- Recognize that emotions disguise and interfere with our ability to be objective in obtaining solutions.
- And lastly but very importantly, trust each other's hearts. Trust that you truly only desire the best for each other. Be peaceful and respectful in discussing your differences, your goals, your vision of the ideal, and learn

from each other. You will both gain from the experience.

Chapter 13: Leadership, Stewardships, and Battleships

I'm going to address some ideas to help you parents, spouses, ecclesiastical leaders, and anyone who is working in some capacity or other that involves making assignments and being responsible for stellar results. Sometimes the choices you make affect your parent-child or your spouse-to-spouse relationship; sometimes your job is on the line, and sometimes your friendship is endangered if your stewardship becomes a battleship. Whatever the situation you are facing, these principles will help you.

Ronald Reagan said, "*The greatest leader is not necessarily the one who does the greatest things. He is the one that gets the people to do the greatest things.*"

I have a personal mantra: *A step outside of your comfort zone is a step into your miracle zone.* It isn't comfortable to be a leader, especially to be a good leader. It isn't comfortable to be a wise steward. It's easier, although much less productive, to be caught up in chaos with emotion, and power grabbing, and ego, and being right. But if

you master the skills of leadership,

you learn how to communicate and delegate stewardship, and

you can experience synergy in team mastermind effort, you will enter your Miracle Zone.

In the previous chapter, I talked about Great and Not So Great Expectations. This is kind of a continuum on that theme, because once we have created a unity in what we envision for our marriage or our family or whatever other organization we're involved in, we have to sell the whole idea to the kids, or the extended family, or the volunteers, or the employees we supervise.

In the corporate setting, once we have created a mission and vision for our business, we have to sell the idea to the people who work with us and are doing some of the basic work to get things done. In a church setting, leaders may be asked to be responsible for outcomes and have to enlist the help of volunteers, who have ideas of their own, so the risk is there to offend or create disharmony if the whole process is handled incorrectly.

Sometimes it's all a muddle, and we face a deep dilemma if we can't figure out the difference, to be able to turn battleships back into stewardships through masterful leadership.

A minister said, "You see the glory, but you don't know the story." Translated, you see the great results, but you don't know the pain, inefficiency, negotiation, prayer, tears, frustration, forgiveness, and renegotiation that had to take place to get the great results you see. When we look at the finished event, or experience, or happy outcome, we don't know the extent of what it took those in charge to create that outcome.

So, what does STEWARDSHIP mean? The root word, of course, is *steward*, and the ending *-ship* means a condition of, or a state of.

When I think of a steward, I think of the guy who comes in your cabin while you're on the cruise ship, and the steward just kind of jumps out of the closet as soon as you leave your room and cleans your room and leaves a cute little monkey or poodle or swan made out of towels on your bed.

The steward has responsibility for your room. His job is to make sure your room is clean, and he has certain criteria by which he is judged in how well he fulfills his stewardship.

A minister has a stewardship over his or her congregation; to help each member feel loved, wanted, and needed; to make sure the church is clean and well maintained, and to engender a spirit of love, peace, spiritual inspiration, and divine power in worship services. Wise clergy measure the success of their stewardships by how much those results are reflected in their outcomes.

A corporate manager has a stewardship over her team, and also over the results the team is getting. Fulfilling certain criteria from the company managers, investors, or founders, can provide feedback on how managers are fulfilling their stewardships.

We all are stewards over planet earth. Roy T. Bennett said, "*Success is not how high you have climbed, but how you make a positive difference to the world.*"

Being a wise steward means looking carefully at the resources you have (and in people that means looking for
strengths and abilities), learning how to use those in a way
that creates more value for all involved, and extending out to
the world.

Your whole life, you are going to be fulfilling roles as a
steward, or as a leader, whether with your family or in business or in volunteer settings. How you manage your role will
determine whether you triumph with your tribe or face fires
of conflict or battle.

William Arthur Ward said, "*The mediocre teacher tells. The
good teacher explains. The superior teacher demonstrates. The
great teacher inspires.*"

Let's translate that all into the concept of stewardship.
This chapter is really an overview to help you recognize how
stewardship affects everything, from family dynamics to corporate success. I focus on how we can use our stewardships
as parents to create more capable, confident, and contributing
children in our family. Then you can extrapolate from that if
you want to improve the outcomes in your church responsibilities.

I'm going to use an example of our children, who refused
to practice the piano. That's a true story from our family history, and we came up with a solution that worked out beauti-
fully, once we figured out how to assign stewardships correctly
and empower our children to fulfill their responsibilities.

I'll break this down. We have stewardship over our children. We wanted them to develop certain skills that we felt
would serve them well in their teen years as well as when they

became adults. In order to do that, we had to allow them their own stewardship. If we pushed or lectured or hinted or were passive aggressive, or even if we gave them a guilt trip, it would have damaged our relationship with them. We had to figure out a way to lead them into wanting to unite with us in our desire to have them learn to play the piano. They had to OWN their own desire to become what they were capable of. They had to be their own stewards over their choices.

After discussing our options in a spousal council, we went to our kids and discussed it in a family council. "We're not going to bug you about practicing," we said. "We will invest our money that we were paying your piano teacher into you. Here's our proposal: we will give you $5 for each piece you can play perfectly on the piano. We won't remind you to practice. We won't force you in any way. This will be your choice."

The results astounded us! Our kids began competing for time to practice the piano! Seldom did the piano sit without someone practicing on it. They spent countless hours, mastered their skills, and today, most of our eight children can play quite well. Over the years, we paid out a small fraction of what we had paid the piano teacher because we allowed our children to own their own stewardship over their musical prowess.

One of my clients wanted her four-year-old twin daughters to make their beds every day and to accomplish other chores in the home. She showed them how to do it, demonstrated what a well-made bed looked like, and then gave THEM stewardship over their bed making. To her delight, the girls make their beds each morning with pleasure, and they don't come out of their bedroom until they have fulfilled their steward-ship over their room. They find joy in accomplishing their chores and in fulfilling their stewardship well.

Pay close attention, because these examples are significant to each of us in having joy on purpose. A key element in both of the previous examples is that the desired results were clearly defined. Participation is enlisted but not enforced, except through means that both leaders and stewards agreed upon. And everyone benefitted in the positive outcomes.

With some of our children, we took lessons in Kajukenbo, which is a blend of several martial arts, including karate, kick-boxing, and judo. Our sifu, or teacher, taught us the principle of nonresistance. When an attacker lunges at you, you can make very minor movements and step outside the area of aggression. The aggressor's own action then places him or her in a vulnerable state, because they are off-balance, leaving them subject to your counterattack.

A female store manager had several men working beneath her in her department. Some of the men felt they deserved the position and resented her leadership. They subtly under-mined her authority, even mocking her behind her back. As she empowered each member of her department with stew-ardship over their areas, tapping into their expertise, she side-stepped the aggression and neatly created a listening atmosphere, where she paid close attention to their sugges-tions and concerns. The result? Her team members became loyal. The gender barrier was eliminated and each team mem-ber respected her and each other for what they could con-tribute. The synergy of their teamwork was powerful.

Roy T. Bennett said, "*Listen with curiosity. Speak with honesty. Act with integrity. The greatest problem with communication is we don't listen to understand. We listen to reply. When we listen with curiosity, we don't listen with the intent to reply. We listen for what's behind the words.*"

In leadership, it's essential to have team members really be on the same team.

In another example, a father's strong desire to have his daughter play violin well resulted in a breach in the father/daughter relationship. In a similar scenario to our relationship with our kids and their learning to play the piano, he visited with her. What did it look like to her to be successful in playing the violin? What would that take, in terms of hours of practicing, or sacrifices she would have to make, or schedules she would have to follow? He made certain to listen and to hear her fears, her ideas, and her suggestions. He asked her to contemplate all that they discussed and then come to him with her decision. She did that, and they wrote down a "contract," with benefits that they both agreed on that she would earn as she followed her plan. The results? Success! She loves the violin, willingly plays, and is progressing forward in her expertise WITHOUT constant reminders, anger, or manipulation.

Eleanor Roosevelt said, "*To handle yourself, use your head; to handle others, use your heart.*"

When we allow others OWNERSHIP in the decisions to be made, and the implementation of their ideas, they become diligent stewards because they know they are heard and appreciated, and they work with more commitment and enthusiasm.

Here's another experience to help clarify stewardship: In a church setting, a newly widowed lady felt shunned. She got the impression that nobody liked her ideas and felt she was unable to contribute in a meaningful way. But by implementing the principles of good leadership and stewardship, she made others feel appreciated for their ideas and efforts. Instead of waiting to be included or invited, SHE did the including and inviting, owning her love for herself and her desire to make a difference. They responded in turn and gave her credit for what she could contribute. The results were a close-knit team of parishioners, all united in helping one another to serve with greater love and spirit.

What do we do when money is tight? If finances are a challenge, we worry about money limiting our ability to show leadership, or stewardship. But as Steve Goodier said, "*Money is not the only commodity that is fun to give. We can give time, we can give our expertise, we can give our love or simply give a smile. What does that cost? The point is, none of us can ever run out of something worthwhile to give.*"

When a great leader needs and wants to unite a team, she doesn't manipulate, control, dictate, or push her team members to get the desired results. Instead, she builds upon an established relationship of trust. She shows her team members what the desired result is, and then invites them to join her in a mastermind to brainstorm about ways to accomplish the result.

The same is true in a great marriage and in a great family, a great community, a great congregation, a great nation.

J. K. Rowling says, in *Harry Potter and the Deathly Hallows*: *"It is a curious thing, Harry, but perhaps those who are best suited to power are those who have never sought it. Those who, like you, have leadership thrust upon them, and take up the mantle because they must, and find to their own surprise that they wear it well."*

Your most important leadership role lies with your family and those you love. When emotions get in your way, or your ego interferes with reason and collaboration, when you feel like you have to win in order to be successful, you self-sabotage. Instead, think of the big picture: what is it you really want? How would it FEEL inside to experience that? What if you could experience those amazing feeling in conjunction with the others in your family? Or your team?

Chapter 14: That's Not Me

Have you ever wondered why some people are able to accomplish their goals, live a life others only dream of, look amazing all the time, have very little stress (if any at all), become fabulously well-to-do, have blissful marriages, happy families and obedient children, contribute generously to make positive changes in the world around them, and the list goes on?

Common sense tells us that no one has that kind of life going on all the time, and that it might not be real, even if it seems so to you, but some people seem to have it a large percentage of the time. I'm going to spend MY time on this chapter helping you to catch the vision of how this happens and how you can achieve the same things. In fact, this insight came to me so powerfully and profoundly that I am going to be applying this knowledge right along with you. And I guarantee it will work.

Here's what you will learn in this chapter and what it will do, if you choose to apply what I teach you:

- You will create a definite plan for your success, in each and every aspect of your life.
- You will envision and develop the exact plan to accomplish what you desire.
- You will be able to face failure with humor and perspective. You'll understand it and be relaxed about it.
- Your relationships with those you love and people around you will improve.
- Your life circumstances will begin changing for the better immediately.
- You will be able to recognize when you are stuck, why you are stuck, and how to get unstuck.
- You will be empowered to help others who trust your leadership.
- You will see yourself and others as you really are.
- Your life will be liberated from addiction, depression, and hesitancy.
- You will feel, and be, truly alive!

Those are some pretty big promises. Why do I think I can be certain of your results? Because my promises are based upon true principles that have been shown to be accurate for millennia of time, as long as we humans have walked the earth.

First of all, I want to say "thank you" to Bob Proctor, and to Leslie Householder, who have used the basis of my construct to teach the power of the mind for years. I have taken their basic construct and created a new iteration of it, which I'm going to use in this chapter today, because the idea came to me and changed my life.

In my construct, I have drawn a large circle for the "head" of a stick figure. Inside the circle are two horizontal lines, dividing the head into thirds. The rest of the stick figure is a tiny circle, representing the body, with little lines as arms and legs. What we'll focus on is the head, and it represents the brain. The brain encompasses who you are, and that's an important concept in understanding the construct. So your heart, your vision, the functions of your body, all are encompassed in the big circle.

The bottom third of the head is called the Reptilian Brain. My sister didn't like that term at first because it reminded her of snakes and lizards, and she's not far off! But although the name is somewhat distasteful to me as well, I kept it, because this is the brain that functions on an animal level. Its role is to keep you safe, and it will warn you not to go out of the cave because the saber-toothed tiger is waiting for you (whether the risk is real or not). It maintains your heartbeat, your respiratory rate, your temperature, the blood flow and basic functions of your body as well. So it serves a valuable purpose. The Reptilian Brain is great! However, it is also important to recognize that much of the Reptilian Brain operates out of fear. It is also focused on instant gratification. It is the brain that says to you, "You've had a hard day. You deserve to veg out and watch a mindless chick flick and eat brownies." It can be demanding and overwhelming to listen to the Reptilian Brain, because it distracts us from meaningful and purposeful living. It's impossible to experience Joy on Purpose when we operate from the level of the Reptilian Brain. Like an animal, it is focused on the next meal, or the sensory gratification, the pleasure centers.

Because the reptilian brain is entirely focused on self-preservation, it tends to be selfish. But it misleads you into thinking that things that do not serve you are good for you, or they solve a problem. An example is the chick flick that wastes time, or the indulgence in fake food that does not nourish you. It employs procrastination and delays your action of doing things that are truly important, because you might fail, or you might be rejected. It keeps you doing menial, safe, repetitive tasks that never really get you where you want to go.

The second brain is the Reactive Brain. This is the brain I added in my construct, and it is the operative brain that I would estimate 95% of the world uses. The Reactive Brain functions based on outside influences. It focuses on the status quo, the old Popeye comment of "I yam what I yam." It is the brain that says I cannot change, because of (and you fill in the blank there). It is the brain that seeks justification for becoming, or staying, a victim. It is the brain that keeps you stuck, that does not allow you to move forward. It is the brain that says, "hey, I don't like my job. I hate going to work, but I'm going to keep doing it because it pays the bills." Or "I wish I could live in a better house, but this one keeps a roof over our heads so I'm not going to explore other options." The Reactive Brain accepts the doctor's diagnosis, the neighbor's gossip, the latest on CNN, as ultimate TRUTH, and it shifts when public opinion shifts. It buys the Pet Rock, or the Chia Pet, because it's popular. It dresses in whatever is fashionable because that's what the brain sees as the best way to operate.

The Reactive Brain gathers "data" or impressions from the Reptilian Brain, so the two are linked. It can, however, change and progress as it learns, because it can also gather data from the Creative Brain, which I'll tell you about next.

Your Creative Brain is the quintessential masterpiece that is YOU. Your Creative Brain, instead of depending on outside influences, influences the outside. It is your highest self, yourself in truth, and your Self that manifests. You have, within your Creative brain, the power to choose EXACTLY what you choose in your life. You can create the life you dream of, the schedule you dream of, the place to work from, the relationships you love, the service you provide, the body you want, the income you seek, the legacy you leave. The Creative Brain has NO limits. It is infinite. It is eternal. It embodies your perfect YOU. It also has control, not just influence, over your Reactive Brain and your Reptilian Brain. It operates from the place of Rare Faith that causes things to happen that otherwise would not be. It invents, it designs, it creates. It is divine.

Now that I have explained all of that to you, let's go through the promises I made at the beginning, and I'll show you how to harness the knowledge of these three brains to serve you and help you create the life you love and seek.

Promise #1: You will create a definite plan for your success, in each and every aspect of your life.

Part of your power to choose is to choose how to spend your time. If you've read Stephen Covey's book, *The Seven Habits of Highly Effective People*, you may recall the story he told of the jar, the rocks, the pebbles, the sand, and the water.

People who are "too busy" are putting the water into the jar first. This is because it's the easiest answer, the quickest, most fluid approach to filling the jar. The jar, by the way, represents your time or your schedule. Once the water is in, they add the sand, then the pebbles, and by the time the pebbles are in the wet sand, there isn't enough room for the big rocks (which represent the most important tasks to be completed). If you reverse the process, placing the rocks in the jar FIRST, then the pebbles, then the sand, then the water, you find that there is room for all of it. ALL OF IT.

So here's how to apply that with your Creative Brain: write down the things you have to do, the things you would like to do, the things you want to do, and the things you need to do. All of them. This is not a fixed list, but get as much in it as you can. Just do a brain dump of everything that weighs on you because you want it completed. If it's a big rock-sized effort, try breaking it down into steps that make it more doable. For example, if one of my dreams is to play the piano, I could have that as my rock goal, then breaking it down I want to find a good teacher. I want to buy the appropriate books to help me learn. I want a piano. I want a scheduled lesson time. And I want to commit to practicing. For years. I'm not going to have the experience of saying, "My goal is to play the piano," and by the end of the day I cross that off my list.

But by using my Creative Brain to determine that playing the piano is very important to me, I create a space in my life for that to happen. When someone calls and says, "Let's go shopping," or "let's do lunch," and it interferes with my piano lesson or my practice time, I'm not going to say yes to that because my Creative Brain decides that the piano is part of manifesting my highest self. If I gave in on lunch or on shopping, I would be lowering my motivation to the level of the Reactive Brain, which reacts to outside influences, or even the Reptilian Brain, looking for instant gratification at lunch.

Now, not everyone desires to play the piano, and that's part of the beauty of the Creative Brain! It operates in an infinite number of creative variations to reflect the exact YOU. So when you are tempted to say yes to something from a lower brain, you can say to yourself, "That's not me!" Decision made. And that's where the title to this chapter came from.

Promise #2: You will envision and develop the exact plan to accomplish what you desire.

This promise is a corollary to the first promise, but it allows you not to just write down your list of the things you have to do, but also the things you would like to do, the things you want to do, and the things you need to do. This is the list of things you DREAM of doing, you HOPE to accomplish, you have IDEAS to implement, CONNECTIONS to establish. This is your most authentic self in embryo. So again, write it all down. All of it! Then your Creative Brain can be put to use to see ways that you can accomplish your dreams. It will also help you winnow out what is most important, and what you want to start on first. It will help you break it down, just as in the example with the piano. For example, suppose one of your dreams is to follow your family history, go to places where your ancestors lived, and create a journey into the past to help discover your roots. Your Creative Brain can help you choose what you need to do to accomplish your dream, deciding how important it is—how big of a rock—and all the steps to get you there.

Promise #3: You will be able to face failure with humor and perspective. You'll understand it and be relaxed about it. When your Creative Brain is in charge of the other two brains, you have the ability to see the big picture. Since you have set your plans firmly in place, prioritized them, and you are taking action, mountains are moving for you. Setbacks are a part of life, but they also can free you in other ways. Even when your health is compromised, or your finances are low, or you feel trapped in your current situation, your Creative Brain can be put to use to influence outside and change your results. Here's the bottom line with your Creative Brain: it is unlimited! No matter what your current situation, someone, somewhere, has been in the same situation or worse, and triumphed. You can too.

Promise #4: Your relationships with those you love and people around you will improve. Instead of living your life with people who annoy you, offend you, attempt to sabotage your efforts–instead of being underemployed, you can make the determination in your Creative Brain to live up to your highest Self, and by doing that you will see everything improve. When you give unconditional love, those who love you will begin to soften and be safe around you. Even people who have been offensive in the past may change as you shower them with your positive influence. And if they don't—because life is their journey too—your path will adjust and you will move to a higher plane of relationships.

Promise #5: Your life circumstances will begin changing for the better immediately. Because your Creative Brain has vision and perspective, you will begin to look at inconveniences or challenges as opportunities to learn. Your overall attitude will be "I can do this!"

Promise #6—and this is a biggie—You will be able to recognize when you are stuck, why you are stuck, and how to get unstuck. Here's your magic wand: when your Creative Brain sees something that doesn't fit the paradigm you have created, you say to yourself, "THAT'S NOT ME." And you don't go there. If you want a body that is healthy, you say, "That's not me" to the unhealthy temptations you face. It is your Reptilian Brain trying to sell you on instant gratification. But that doesn't work anymore, because it's not you. Your Creative Brain is YOU.

Promise #7: You will be empowered to help others who trust your leadership. People are looking for inspiration, for examples, for torchbearers to lead and guide them on their journey. When others see how you are accomplishing your dreams, they will be led to you and you will be in a position to help because you KNOW it can be done.

Promise #8: You will see yourself and others as you really are. In doing so, you will find yourself in a place of peace; a place of confidence that knows exactly what is YOU, your wonderful SELF, and what is a false brain prompting something that is inconsistent and dishonest to your SELF.

Promise #9: Your life will be liberated from addiction, depression, and hesitancy. A major part of moving forward is knowing who YOU are and knowing what it true about you.

Freeing yourself from these reptilian fears will put you in a place to create your results instead of resigning yourself to suffering and pain.

And lastly, but not least, **Promise #10**: You will feel, and be, truly alive!

I want to tell you a true story . . . and for this story there are countless others that you can read to inspire you. This story is about Kyle Maynard, a congenital quadruple amputee who was born without arms or legs. On January 15, 2012, Maynard became the first quadruple amputee to climb Mount Kilimanjaro without assistance, by crawling all 19,340 feet in just 10 days. I heard Kyle speak and I was mesmerized by his commitment to his dream. Nothing would stop him. And nothing did. Kyle said, "Every person on the planet has a disability—not just those we can see. And we all choose whether we allow our lives to be defined by them or not."

Another amazing climber reached the summit of Mount Everest in 2018 at the age of 69. Four decades after losing his feet to frostbite on Mount Everest, a Chinese double amputee became the first person to conquer the world's highest peak without legs from the Nepal side.

With the accomplishment, Xia Boyu became the first double amputee to scale the mountain from Nepal territory.

In 1975, Xia lost both feet to severe frostbite after giving a sick teammate his sleeping bag during a failed Everest bid while on the Chinese national mountaineering team. Two decades later, both of his legs below the knee were amputated after he developed a rare form of blood cancer.

"I love the mountain," Xia said before the climb. "I will fight for it my entire life."

During his previous attempts in 2014, 2015, and 2016, Xia's unsuccessful tries to beat Everest were scuttled by a series of natural disasters, including an avalanche, a 7.8-magnitude earthquake, and a blizzard that forced him to turn back just 300 feet from the summit.

My goals and dreams do not include mountain climbing, but seeing these men be true to their highest Self and follow their dreams inspires me! What are the mountains you want to climb? How can you prepare? How will you deal with the obstacles that inevitably will be part of your journey? And most important: which brain will you allow to govern this, your only life. This is your only chance to manifest YOU as YOURSELF, as your highest SELF, as your ONLY self, and leave the world the legacy that only you can give.

Climb your mountains, my friends. Live your dream! And be true to your highest self that is manifested through your Creative Brain.

And remember:

Your life is all about learning, growing, and experiencing the joy all around you. Let it seep in, let your heart embrace it and your mind and eyes feast on it. Fill your heart with gratitude that you have the chance to experience this, and that you have people in your life to love and learn from. No matter how busy you are, take a minute to make a difference. And savor the perfection in every precious moment.

Chapter 15: Day-to-Day Decisions and Destiny

In one day, three of my clients approached me for coaching help about three completely different issues; one, regarding disappointment in business; the second, about disappointment in love; and the third, how to have healthy family relationships. But the solutions to their difficult situations are all based on the same principles: Our day-to-day decisions determine our destiny.

Henry Emerson Fosdick, an insightful Protestant minister, said, "*The tragic evils of our life are so commonly unintentional. We did not start out for that poor, cheap goal. That aim was not in our hearts at all; . . . that is why the road to hell is always paved with good intentions. and that is why I am not celebrating high ideals, lofty aims, fine purposes, grand resolutions, but am saying instead that one of the most dangerous things in the world is to accept them and think you believe in them and then neglect the day-by-day means that lead to them. Ah, my soul, look to the road you are walking on! He who picks up one end of the stick picks up the other. He who chooses the beginning of a road chooses the place it leads to. It is the means that determines the end."*

When I coach, I don't usually provide the answers to a situation or challenge. You have the ability to tap into your Self and find the answers within you.

Why is it such a challenge to follow through on the actions, attitudes, and activities that get us where we want to go? In *Alice in Wonderland*, the Cheshire Cat asks Alice where she is going and she doesn't have an answer for him.

"Would you tell me, please, which way I ought to go from here?"

"That depends a good deal on where you want to get to," said the Cat.

"I don't much care where—" said Alice.

"Then it doesn't matter which way you go," said the Cat.

"—so long as I get somewhere," Alice added as an explanation.

"Oh, you're sure to do that," said the Cat, "if you only walk long enough."

Today I'm going to share with you the model that I have come up with, that creates a bridge from where you are to where you want to be. To cross that bridge requires some pretty significant thought and prayer. You need to be able to take the time to really explore what is important to you. You need to be able to get right down to the nitty-gritty of who you are and what you want out of this, your only life. This process may require some pretty intense soul searching, even to the point of facing things from the past that have stunted your progress. Just remember, the past may have put you where you are now, but it does NOT define your present, OR your future. You have absolute ownership over what you choose to do in your present. The past can be instructive, but it does not dictate your present. YOU do. Your future is also up to you, and this model will help you to get there.

One of the cool things about this model is it spells "S-T-R-E-A-M" and it gets you across that bridge to your next model. Your next model is what you get when you have gotten past the barriers to where you want to be, and you are ready to D-R-E-A-M and make your ultimate goals happen. For now, let's focus on the first model, STREAM, that gets you from where you are to where you want to be.

Your impressions are based upon what you SEE. The S in See is the first letter in the acronym STREAM. One "eye" site (get it?) describes vision in this way: In a normal eye, the light rays come to a sharp focusing point on the retina. The retina functions much like the film in a camera. ... The retina receives the image that the cornea focuses through the eye's internal lens and transforms this image into electrical impulses that are carried by the optic nerve to the brain.

This summer, my husband's retina became detached in one of his eyes and had to be surgically reattached. He first noticed a problem when the ground at his feet seemed wavy and uneven, although he knew that wasn't the case. The detachment and repair have significantly changed his vision, and we won't know for at least six months how much it will ultimately affect his eyesight.

Here's my point: what we SEE may not necessarily be what

IS. But we use our sight as a tool to help us understand where we are.

Next letter in the model is T, and that stands for THOUGHTS. When we SEE something, we have THOUGHTS about what we see. Our thoughts help us to begin to interpret what our eyes show us is happening around us.

The third letter in the model is R, which stands for RE-SPONSE. Our response is an immediate assessment of what we have seen and what our thoughts tell us. It happens even before we have any feelings about it. It just is a flash of impression that comes to us as we see things. Most of what we see does not evoke any emotion at all. It just is, and it just happens around us constantly. But once we have THOUGHTS about what we SEE, and we RESPOND to what we think, we begin to have emotions.

We assign EMOTIONS to our response, which then affect our

ACTIONS, which results in

MANIFESTATION

S-T-R-E-A-M

We see a picture on a wall. The picture itself has no emotions tied to it, but it is a picture of a cabin where we had fun as a child, or broke our arm playing there, the picture that our eyes (1) SEE generates (2) THOUGHTS, which bring about a response: in this case, either a positive (3) RESPONSE thinking about the fun, or a more negative response thinking about the broken arm. Either of those responses will evoke

(4) EMOTION, which then generates (5) ACTION and (6) MANIFESTATION.

The process of the model happens very quickly–sometimes instantaneously, and it isn't always in sequence. When we feel stuck, it's a good idea to take time to recognize each step of the model and how we can adjust our thoughts, responses, and emotions to affect our actions and the ultimate manifestation of our experience. A coach can help with that.

The significant part is that we assign meaning to what we see, based on our EMOTIONS and THOUGHTS and RESPONSES to what we see.

If four people are standing on different corners of an intersection when an accident occurs, police will get four completely different stories on what happened. Why is this? Because of PERSPECTIVE. Breaking the model down in our Creative Brain allows us to see that what OUR eyes see may not be the complete picture, especially when we take the time to assess our thoughts, responses, and emotions BEFORE we take action and results manifest.

So what's the takeaway here? It is that we are constantly SEEing what is going on around us, but what we SEE isn't necessarily good or bad; it's the meaning we place on it. This happens all the time in social media, where people are making diametrically opposed claims on politics, or climate change, or scientific proof, or medicine. Each person is just as passionate as the other. Each may be SEEING the same thing, but because of perspective: emotion, response, and thoughts, in whatever order, they take different ACTION.

This can be a very helpful model to you when you start to

experience strong emotions. You can even quiet down anxiety or panic if you can calm your brain to take each step of the model and evaluate your own unique processing of each step carefully.

Now let's take the model and use it to get us where Alice in Wonderland didn't know she wanted to go: a positive place, where we can be whole, and safe, and happy, and enjoying life in all its amazing splendor. This can be a place where even amazing miracles happen, or wild dreams come true, just because we, knowingly or unknowingly, apply the principles in this chapter.

I share this experience with permission. Two years ago, we took a trip to Italy with our son and daughter-in-law and their family. To say it was magical is an understatement. Our son Joel made some plans that were absolutely off the chart in terms of a dream trip. He scheduled an AirBandB in a lovely spot that overlooked St. Peter's Square in Vatican City. He arranged for a nighttime tour of the Coliseum. He got tickets for a breakfast at the Vatican, and we had a special tour of the Sistine Chapel. But the most memorable experience was seeing the Pope in person at St. Peter's Square in one of the Wednesday addresses he makes whenever he is in Rome.

I am not a member of the Catholic Church, but I have enormous respect for the Pope. So there we were, members of The Church of Jesus Christ of Latter-day Saints, planning a trip to go see and hear the Pope, along with somewhere around 5,000 other people.

People save for years to make what for many is the trip of a lifetime. Couples come dressed in their wedding clothes, hoping to catch the Pope's eye and receive his personal blessing upon their marriage. People bring their handicapped loved ones in hopes the Pope will bless and heal them. Parents dress their babies in special clothes, wanting the Pope to bless and kiss their babies.

Joel and Heather had laughingly talked about their youngest son, our grandson Spencer, who was then eight years old but very small for his age. They had envisioned how fun it would be to put a pacifier in his mouth and dress him up like a baby so the Pope could bless him and kiss him. They just put it out there and did not attach emotion to the idea. It was mostly just a fun idea.

On the way from the U.S. to Rome, Joel happened to sit next to a Catholic priest, Father Alex. Father Alex told Joel that if we were going to see the Pope, there was a best place to sit that had the most chance of seeing him up close when he went by. There would be about 5,000 people in the square, each hoping for a close-up glimpse of the Pope.

So when the morning came for our papal audience visit, Joel, my husband Stan, and I went early to St. Peter's Square and got our seats. I was stunned when Joel selected a spot that was in the back in the corner, not front and center like everybody else was doing.

Pay attention to these little hints: no emotional attachment, not doing what everybody else is doing, and acting on the "coincidences" that show up.

Heather and the kids joined us in the seats, and we watched and listened, enthralled, as several men played a short alphorn, or Swiss alpenhorn, concert. These are the really cool, super-long horns that you see on the packages of Ricola cough drops.

It was so impressive! Then a few dignitaries spoke briefly, and some beautiful prayers were spoken, hymns sung. Pope Francis delivered a wonderful, inspiring address. Shortly thereafter, he climbed into his specially designed vehicle called the "Popemobile." Surrounded by his secret service men and members of the Swiss Guard, the Popemobile began slowly driving around the crowd.

The visual effects of his travel around the area were stunning. The Swiss Guard uniform design stems from the Renaissance Period, and they look almost like court jesters with the multicolored stripes and flounces. But the Swiss Guard are some of the world's most highly trained marksmen, and their mission is to protect the Pope. They do this very well.

We watched, excited along with the crowd, as the Popemobile wove in and around the area. Suddenly it turned behind us and began making its way toward our corner! Collectively, we held our breath as we watched the vehicle get closer and closer. Our grandson JD held Spencer up on the barricade fence so he could see. And, almost in disbelief, we watched as Pope Francis's eyes lit upon Spencer, and he gave a slight nod. The Secret Service man came over to where we were standing, picked Spencer up, and carried him over to the Pope. With great tenderness, the Pope laid his hands upon our Spencer and kissed him. Then the Secret Service man brought him back.

It took probably just a couple of minutes for that entire event to transpire, but time seemed to stop. Had we really just seen that happen? We were shaking and crying and hugging each other, tears streaming down our faces. This little family from Utah, from another religion, but having great love and respect for Pope Frances, had just experienced something incredible.

The people around us hugged us and cried with us. The Pope's photographer handed us a card so we could get a photograph of that moment. I've posted it in my blogsite, cristiegardner.com. Wow! It was magical. It was momentous. It was life changing. And it was transformational.

I believe God gives us moments to experience miraculous events so we recognize His laws in effect. Moreover, I believe those moments can happen again and again, with greater frequency, when we understand, apply, and tap into His laws.

When we live our lives ON PURPOSE, we can affect, to a large extent, the results we desire. This happens when we recognize and apply the model with increasing focus and experience.

I'll be sharing much, much more about God's laws and how we can apply them to our benefit during the course of these chapters. I'm so grateful to know HE is mindful of me. He is mindful of Spencer, and his family, and the Pope, and all of the wonderful people who were with us in St. Peter's Square that day, and all of his children and the creatures around the world.

Let's review this model in context:

Joel and Heather "SAW" the possibility of Spencer being blessed by the Pope.

They "THOUGHT" how fun it would be, but they didn't attach to it.

They "RESPONDED" openly when circumstances opened up, such as Father Alex sitting next to Joel. This one is important because Joel could have insisted he sit next to someone in his family or stayed silent and sulked during the flight. Instead, he took the opportunity to connect with Father Alex and ask him about Italy.

EMOTIONS were positive and excited, without any attachment to a certain outcome.

Joel took ACTION to sit where Father Alex indicated was the best spot to see the Pope. The desired outcome, however amazing and impossible it seemed, MANIFESTED.

You can do the exact same things to bring about change and miracles in your life, as you link with God and follow His laws. This requires faith, actually Rare Faith, that causes things to happen which otherwise would not be. And D-R-E-A-M keeps the same final four steps, but it begins with DE-SIRE and DECIDE, which is your next path in creating your desired results.

"Your task, to build a better world," God said. I answered, "How? The world is such a large vast place, so complicated now. And I so small and useless am, there's nothing I can do. But God in all His wisdom said, "Just build a better you."

If you are feeling discouraged, if you have a giant dream or goal that seems impossible, take the time to really explore this model and how it can help you achieve what you desire.

Chapter 16: Dangerous Underminings

Butte, Montana, is a very interesting place. Said by many to be the most heavily mined ground in the world, Butte sits atop an estimated 7,000 miles of abandoned mine tunnels and smelting waste pits that have since slowly filled with a neon blue "plume" of toxic wastewater in an aquifer 50 to 60 feet below the surface.

It is home to more than 200 mines dug years ago that undermined "The Hill" and its surrounding neighborhoods. Mine shafts crisscross much of the central district of Butte. An interesting result of the mines is the superfund site, the Berkeley Pit, which is a remnant of what went seriously wrong when man went against nature in a greedy grasp for precious metals, without consideration for the fallout. The pit is the result of mines being flooded and the end result is a very toxic body of water. It is so toxic that birds flying over it or drinking from it will die. It is an eerie, strange testament to poorly executed plans without consideration of the toxic consequences.

Our family visited Butte several years ago. Walking

through the central district, we could peek through cracks in the sidewalks and see dozens, and sometimes hundreds, of feet down, into the mining shafts. Occasionally the sidewalk foundations fail, and sinkholes appear, revealing uncharted mine shafts, sometimes swallowing parts of cars or opening up in backyards, risking injury to people passing by.

It was in Butte that I really began to understand the meaning of the word *undermine*. The entire central district is undermined with shafts that crisscross and intersect, forming a web of tunnels. With those giant tunnels, sometimes, the earth beneath the town shifts—not dramatically, but enough that sidewalks crack, buildings tilt and windows don't quite shut properly. The most concerning problem, however, happens each spring, when unregulated vertical shafts dug in the early days of exploring the area's mineral resources appear in surprising places.

Because they were dug before any kinds of regulations were in place, you may not see the shafts on a map. They were dug in the 1870s and 1880s. When miners were finished with those access points, they covered the holes with thick boards and filled in with dirt. Now, hundreds of years later, the boards are rotting and when the ground thaws, depressions form in several places around the city, sometimes opening up a man-made sinkhole, sometimes showing planks of rotting timber reemerging from the ground.

At one time, over 100,000 people lived in Butte and the surrounding areas. Now, there are about 34,000 inhabitants, about one-third its previous population. Metaphorically speaking, this is indicative of what happens when undermining takes place. Let me explain. To do that, I'm going to segue to a few other symbolically applicable analogies.

I hired a trainer to help me achieve my fitness goals, and one of the first things he worked on with me was my balance. He had me stand on a Bosu ball, a curved half-ball shape that is secured onto a flat base. I had to stand, first with both feet on the ball, then with one foot in the air and the other adjusting constantly to keep me upright. Then he had me switch feet. He taught me how important it is to have a firm foundation, and then to stay balanced. The hundreds of small muscles in my legs and feet learned to maintain the balance with the challenge of staying upright on a curved surface.

It's important to realize the connection between having a good understanding and what happens when the foundation isn't solid beneath us, when undermining takes place. People haven't used the word *undermining* as much lately, Undermining has several different meanings, all related:

- to injure or destroy by insidious activity or imperceptible stages, sometimes tending toward a sudden dramatic effect.
- to attack by indirect, secret, or underhand means; attempting to subvert by stealth.
- to make an excavation under; dig or tunnel beneath, as a military stronghold.
- to weaken or cause to collapse by removing underlying support, as by digging away or eroding the foundation.

Undermining can happen in friendships; it can happen in

relationships with our spouse or loved ones. It can, and often does, happen in work situations. Often it stems from jealousy or insecurity on the part of the one who is doing the undermining.

The *Journal of Organizational Behavior* defines undermining as:

Behavior intended to hinder, over time, the ability to establish and maintain positive interpersonal relationships, work-related success, and favorable reputation.

When someone undermines you, or your credibility, or your authority, it is sometimes difficult to recognize immediately. Undermining can be disguised as a backhanded compliment, or a passive-aggressive remark that at first just causes slight twinges of discomfort, and then upon reflection strikes you as cruel and demeaning. You may feel as though you have to constantly be on the defensive when you are around an underminer. They may disguise gossip as concerns, or they may view you as competition. Sometimes they gain power over you by tempting you in an area where you are weak, such as offering you a goodie when you have already made it clear you are wanting to eat healthier.

At any rate, people who undermine can cause a good deal of stress and anxiety for us, and they can make us feel as though we have something to prove.

Here are some pithy comments that apply to undermining:

Bishop TD Jakes said, "*When you are a giraffe and you receive criticism from turtles, they are reporting the view from the level they are on.*" Everyone is on a different level. If someone does something that is beneath you, don't stoop to their level.

Steve Maraboli says, "*Know your circle. Make sure everybody in your 'boat' is rowing and not drilling holes when you're not looking.*" And to that I add, if the kind of "friends" who surround you are like that, don't hesitate to bail on the friendship!

People can hide undermining with sarcasm. They can say something unkind or judgmental, and then make the half-hearted disclaimer, "Just kidding." Well, really, they're not kidding. Kidding is plain and simple meanness. It has NO place in our interactions or conversations with other human beings. Especially with children, teenagers, or people who are not on a similar social or cultural scale.

So how do we handle the person who undermines us? The stresses and pain and embarrassment can be devastating. How do we stop it? I'm going to share some thoughts to help get our emotions into a place where we can approach the issue rationally, and then we'll take the whole concept through my model for achieving our desired end results.

One way to get past the pain of someone who undermines us is to look carefully for possible motives. Jealousy is certainly an option, in which case we can feel somewhat flattered rather than threatened by an undermining insult. Our son dealt with an issue from another boy who was not only jealous, but verbally and physically abusive. To add insult to injury, this boy, in his early tweens, invited all the young people within their circle to a birthday party but deliberately excluded our son.

Of course, I responded as the mama bear looking out for

her cub! I wanted to confront the kid, go talk to his parents, and get the whole thing straightened out! But that would not have solved the issue. In fact, I was at odds trying to figure out what would.

Let's think about my model: S-T-R-E-A-M. Stream stands for what we SEE, then the THOUGHTS that creates, followed by our immediate RESPONSE. Our response triggers EMOTIONS, which then lead to our ACTION and the resultant MANIFESTATION.

Interestingly, it was our son that solved the issue, but I'm going to take you through my (very) inadequate reactions first. I SAW that someone had attacked my child. I THOUGHT it was WAY out of line and unjust, even unwarranted. My RESPONSE was that this kid was being a real bully and jerk, and it roused strong negative, angry EMOTIONS in me.

Now here's where it gets interesting. Because I recognized the EMOTIONS were destructive and would not achieve any kind of positive result, I made another choice. I did not take ACTION, and so none of my negative MANIFESTATIONS occurred.

Here's what we did. Our son visited with us about the whole scenario in a family council. We reviewed possible actions he could take in dealing with the underminer who had attacked him. But we honestly couldn't think of a proactive, win-win solution! We asked our son to pray about it and come back with some ideas.

He did so, and when he came back, he was smiling. He asked if I had a birthday card he could use, and he put a

$10 bill, his own money, inside. He went up to the bully and handed him the card. He said, "I heard it was your birthday. Happy Birthday!" The bullying stopped. The undermining stopped. And to a certain extent, the bully turned into a friend. I loved that our son did not stoop to the level of a "turtle." He chose to be a "giraffe" and to look at the whole issue from a higher standpoint. Or, using the other analogy, he was busy plugging the holes that the other guy drilled in his jealousy.

In an earlier chapter, I talked about our Kajukenbo class, where we were taught to step sideways out of the way of an attacking aggressor. This allows the momentum of the aggressor to carry them forward, off balance, and makes them more vulnerable. That is exactly what our son's unexpected kindness did. Instead of an angry reaction, he chose the higher ground. Some might think that giving a gift to the bully was a form of ransom, but it was a gesture made with a kind heart and no judgment. People can sense that.

Ralph Waldo Emerson said,

"What you do speaks so loudly that I cannot hear what you say."

Sometimes the person doing the undermining is the first one to see it in others and the last one to notice it in his or her self. Here are some things to look for to determine if you are undermining your spouse or other people. If the whole relationship makes you uneasy, and you can't quite put a finger on what is happening and how to deal with it, try putting pen to paper and just write down absolutely everything going through your mind, related or not. In doing a "brain dump," you will see some patterns emerge and you will be able to be more logical and strategic in how to deal with your circumstances.

Parents:

- Do you openly disagree with your spouse in front of the children?
- Do you give a different answer when your spouse gives or does not give permission to the children?
- Do you tell your children "wait until your [mom or dad] gets home?
- Do you use your child as a go-between to relay information to your spouse?
- Do you change the consequences your spouse has already given for behavior?
- Do you argue in front of the children?
- Do you allow your child to break rules your spouse has set? This one is problematic if parents have not already set the rules together, with the family, in family council.
- Do you complain about your spouse with friends in front of your children?
- Do you take the blame for your child's mistakes?
- Do you tell your child not to tell your spouse something?

In a business or professional setting, learn to be proactive about undermining. You can start with a simple conversation. For example, if you were not invited to a meeting, you address that out loud and let the person who did not include you know that you were sure it was an oversight, but please include you in the future. This is a subtle, but effective, way to establish your fair-mindedness, and also puts the offender on notice, all while making it clear to everyone what is happening.

When you take the tiger by the tail in a direct, kind way, it eliminates the power that the person undermining has assumed over you. Just be careful to avoid being confrontational when you are faced with a similar situation.

Avoid being overly friendly if you are aware of someone who undermines. Keep your accomplishments and successes to yourself, or share them only with trusted friends and family who honor your efforts.

Most importantly, focus on the good. What you focus on expands.

When people make comments that are jealous or demeaning, you can minimize your reaction. For example, "I can't believe you're trying to get into that program. Don't you know how hard it is?" You can listen selectively to what they say and respond to the question or comment they should have said. A mild response such as "Well, nothing ventured, nothing gained" can often stop the assault.

In dealing with underminers, keep your own ego under control. Our ego jumps to unnecessary conclusions that do not serve us when we face a confrontation from an underminer.

For example, if they say, "You should get another couch.

This one is so uncomfortable!" You can respond with, "Yes, I'd love a new couch!" or "Wouldn't that be awesome!"

Passive-aggressive behavior is another way that people can undermine. So is micromanaging. If your underminer is a casual acquaintance or a colleague, it's easy enough to just stop talking to them. But with a friend or family member, it's not so easy.

When friends or family start using undermining in their interactions with you, consider giving the friendship a break. Don't spend as much time with them and let your spirit heal. Start working on all the lovely goals you have for yourself. Enjoy the solitude. Change the relationship so that you are not as vulnerable.

As William Shakespeare said in Othello,

Good name in man and woman, dear my lord,
Is the immediate jewel of their souls:
Who steals my purse steals trash; 'tis something, nothing;
'twas mine, 'tis his, and has been slave to thousands;
But he that filches from me my good name
Robs me of that which not enriches him,
And makes me poor indeed.

It's important to steer clear of judging others. But if the offenses keep coming, and you can't figure out a way around them, try to find a "righteous" reason for their behavior. My mom used to always say, "Oh their husband (or wife) didn't kiss them goodbye this morning," or "Maybe they are in a really tough situation and can't figure a way out." Shannon Alder said, "*Hide yourself in God, so when a man wants to find you he will have to go there first.*"

Lastly, watch your own conversations carefully to make sure you are a support and strength to others instead of an underminer. You can be honest and still be kind. You can lift others and still maintain your own level of growth. You can be sure of your own foundation and balance being strong. And when you are strong and confident on your own, you will find yourself able to take others' underminings with a grain of salt. No one can replace the one and only YOU!

17

Chapter 17: Maximum Performance with Minimal Stress

An American investment banker was at the pier of a small coastal Mexican village when a small boat with just one fisherman docked. Inside the small boat were several large yellow fin tuna. The American complimented the Mexican on the quality of his fish and asked how long it took to catch them.

The Mexican replied, "only a little while."

The American then asked why didn't he stay out longer and catch more fish? The Mexican said he had enough to support his family's immediate needs.

The American then asked, "but what do you do with the rest of your time?"

The Mexican fisherman said, "I sleep late, fish a little, play with my children, take siestas with my wife, Maria, stroll into the village each evening where I sip wine, and play guitar with my amigos. I have a full and busy life."

The American scoffed, "I am a Harvard MBA and could help you. You should spend more time fishing and with the proceeds, buy a bigger boat. With the proceeds from the bigger boat, you could buy several boats, eventually you would have a fleet of fishing boats. Instead of selling your catch to a middleman you would sell directly to the processor, eventually opening your own cannery. You would control the product, processing, and distribution. You would need to leave this small coastal fishing village and move to Mexico City, then LA and eventually New York City, where you will run your expanding enterprise."

The Mexican fisherman asked, "But, how long will this all take?"

To which the American replied, "15–20 years.

"But what then?" asked the Mexican.

The American laughed and said, "That's the best part. When the time is right you would announce an IPO and sell your company stock to the public and become very rich, you would make millions!"

"Millions—then what?"

The American said, "Then you would retire. Move to a small coastal fishing village where you would sleep late, fish a little, play with your kids, take siestas with your wife, stroll to the village in the evenings where you could sip wine and play your guitar with your amigos."

Benjamin Franklin said, "Dost thou love life? Then do not squander time, for that is the stuff life is made of."

Our son started a nonprofit in Africa. He told us that the people have basically nothing, but they are happy. Children spend hours creating their own toys: soccer balls out of discarded plastic bags; toy cars and trucks out of fencing material. I have noticed the same in the Philippines, and in Guatemala, where time is enjoyed in the present moment. People take painstaking effort to create beautiful crafts, with outstanding workmanship, and find peace and pleasure in their efforts. In the happiest of cultures, time is most often experienced in the present, enjoying the NOW without worry about the past or fear of the future. It seems as though they intuitively understand what Lao Tzu meant when he said, "*Nature does not hurry, yet everything is accomplished.*"

Philip DeFranco said, "*The fact that you are even here, alive, on this planet is a mathematical miracle, and you should not spend the time that you have being busy being miserable.*"

Life is a magical adventure. Yet it comes with seemingly contradictory rules for success: take time for loved ones but schedule your days and weeks for maximum accomplishments, plan your life in detail, yet live with spontaneity. Stay focused on the big picture and don't go off course, but stop when someone needs your help in a crisis. Put yourself first and yet serve others. Do what you don't want to do for a few years so you can live like you want for the rest of your life. Where in the world is time for all of that?

There isn't. So what do we do?

Alabama wrote a country song with these lyrics in the chorus:

I'm in a hurry to get things done
Oh I rush and rush until life's no fun
All I really gotta do is live and die
But I'm in a hurry and don't know why.

When we talk about joy, fulfilling our purpose, living deliberately, making wise choices, we sometimes feel over-whelmed and almost paralyzed. How do we deal with the frustrations and challenges of daily life without losing our focus, our momentum?

There are days we feel like we are on top of the world, quickly followed by days where we feel like we are in a stupor, unable to get anything done. At times it seems that every step forward is followed by two steps back.

We all know the value of planning. But what happens when it seems like life hits us sideways and we don't know which way to go from upside down? Getting ready for a trip, packing in a frenzy at the last minute. Showing up at the airport without our ID, our phone charger, our toothbrush. Have you ever done any of that?

A client told me that when she was putting off a task she needed to do, or she didn't know how to prioritize her time, her house got really clean! She knew how to scrub bathrooms and fold laundry. But when facing a job that required some research, some planning, some creative brain effort, she started cleaning.

Day after day, we use our time to accomplish the quick and easy tasks, the mindless jobs that we like to do or we can do easily, while we shove off the projects that would really change our lives if we put them first. We allow ourselves to get distracted.

I remember when my beloved brother-in-law passed away, way too young, at the age of 26. As we were preparing to go to his funeral, I found myself suddenly choosing to sew lace onto the edges of pillowcases. I think my mind and my spirit needed something that didn't require thinking, trying to avoid the pain of grieving his loss.

So, as James Gleick says, "*We go back and forth between being time's master and its victim.*"

Why and how does this happen? My personal opinion is that we really are dwelling in the illusion of time, but it doesn't come naturally to us, because we are eternal beings. So when we move into the dimension of time at birth, we have to learn a concept that is completely foreign. We are constantly making adjustments, living in a framework that our spirits do not understand, trying to make sense of this one and only life we live. We recognize the value of each moment, but we can get lost in the frantic effort to make each moment meaningful. As Art Buchwald said, "*Whether it's the best of times or the worst of times, it's the only time we've got.*"

Make no mistake: it is VERY important to recognize and come to an understanding of our relationship with time. But, as Michael Altshuler said, "*The bad news is time flies. The good news is you're the pilot.*"

Speaking of this adventure we call life, Dieter F. Uchtdorf said, "*If you hesitate in this adventure because you doubt your ability, remember that discipleship is not about doing things perfectly, it is about doing things intentionally. It is your choices that show what you truly are, far more than your abilities.*"

So then, the answer lies in what we INTEND to do with our time and how truly we honor our choice by fulfilling our intentions.

President Dwight D. Eisenhower used a matrix to help him meet his time goals with intention instead of regret. The matrix is a quadrant. Stephen Covey expanded on the quadrant concept to include helpful descriptions of what should fill the quadrants.

In the upper left corner of the quadrant is the "*Urgent*" category. Eisenhower captioned this quadrant, "*DO.*" Covey expanded to explain that this includes medical emergencies, crises, and deadline-driven projects. The contents of the *Urgent* quadrant are the absolute necessities.

In the upper right is the "*Not Urgent, but Important*" category, Eisenhower captioned the contents "*Plan.*" Covey explained: Personal Fulfillment is the descriptor. This quadrant includes our health, exercise, relationships, and personal growth.

Our objective is to address the areas in the "*Not Urgent, but Important*" quadrant, thus preventing so many issues that pop up in the *Urgent* quadrant. The bottom left quadrant is the "*Not Important, but Urgent*" category. Eisenhower captioned this quadrant: *Delegate.* Covey expounded to include: Distractions, Interruptions, Phone Calls, and most Meetings to fill this quadrant.

The fourth quadrant, on the lower right, is *Not Urgent, Not Important*, Eisenhower captioned *Eliminate.* Covey placed Time Wasters, such as Trivial Busywork, Junk Mail, Mindless games, and TV shows, in the *Not Urgent, Not Important* quadrant.

When our brain is fatigued with wasted time or is overwhelmed, it wants us to move into the Time Wasters quadrant. We give it an illusion of purpose, such as watching TV, pretending we are spending time with loved ones, or constantly cleaning our house, or in my case, sewing lace onto pillowcases, but in reality it is just an excuse to try to fool ourselves into thinking we are not wasting our precious time.

The Eisenhower Matrix can be a valuable tool to help us differentiate between what is demanding our attention with urgency and how we really want to spend our lives, with what is not urgent but important. The more of our goals that we fit into the Important quadrant, the happier we are; and the more purposefully we spend our time. I have designed a model that is available to my coaching clients which explains this and helps clarify even more how to allocate our time.

When our minds are stuck in a stupor and we can't differentiate between what is urgent or important, and what are distractions and time wasters, we can use this matrix to help us get centered again.

When you use the matrix, it may take extra time at first. But once you have mastered the matrix, your decisions will become clearer and more instantaneous.

An ounce of morning is worth a pound of afternoon. So if you can begin your day early, having already differentiated between what is urgent and what is important, you will triumph over your time on a more regular basis. You will begin to see yourself accomplish your goals, and you will gain greater confidence in yourself.

Carl Sandburg said, "*Time is the coin of your life. It is the only coin you have, and only you can determine how it will be spent. Be careful lest you let other people spend it for you.*" Steve Jobs echoed that thought when he said, "*Your time is limited, so don't waste it living someone else's life.*"

Mastering the matrix puts you in the captain's seat, and you are no longer subject to other peoples' requests and demands on your time. When you make a choice to spend time, you schedule it and live into your plan. Amazingly, time opens up so you can be more spontaneous and enjoy life more fully with the people you care about.

Be sure to plan also for "unplanned" time–that is, time to handle the unexpected, and as Goethe said, " *Every second is of infinite value.*" If your unexpected time allotment doesn't fill up, you have the added gift of time to spend however you choose.

If you're beating yourself up about the time you have wasted in the past, cheer up. A Chinese proverb says, "*The best time to plant a tree was 20 years ago. The second best time is now.*" And the wise Mother Theresa said, "*Yesterday is gone. Tomorrow has not yet come. We have only today. Let us begin.*"

I'm really proud of my sister, who decided after her children were all grown that she wanted to complete her bachelor's degree. It wasn't easy, and it wasn't urgent, but it was important to her. She struggled, and she studied, and she made time to accomplish her goal. From there she has gone on to other dreams, including participating in an archaeological dig. Steve Jobs said, "*My favorite things in life don't cost any money. It's really clear that the most precious resource we all have is time.*"

One of my clients told me, "I'm too old to begin now! Think how old I'll be if I try to do this!" My response was, "think how old you'll be if you don't do this!"

Napoleon Hill said, "*Don't wait. The time will never be just right.*" And Earl Nightingale said, "*Don't let the fear of the time it will take to accomplish something stand in the way of your doing it. The time will pass anyway; we might just as well put that passing time to the best possible use.*"

I remember when my eight children were growing up at home and I felt like I had to run to get everything done. Meals were huge! The kids drank 17 gallons of milk a week, so shopping was always a massive effort. Laundry was mountainous. I never finished. Ever. But my work then was important; really important. I would not exchange the precious hours cooking, cleaning, and folding, for a high income in the corporate world.

Why? Because in those moments I got hugs, tears, snuggles, and high fives. I bandaged owies and listened to my children struggle through tough times. I was able to help shape decisions and change the course of their lives. That time is gone now. But the memories feed my soul, especially as I watch them do the same with their children.

Thoreau asked, "*Why should we live with such hurry and waste of life?*" And his thoughtful question is answered with this beautiful insight of Francis Bacon: "*Begin doing what you want to do now. We are not living in eternity. We have only this moment, sparkling like a star in our hand—and melting like a snowflake.*"

Emily Dickinson said, "*Forever is composed of nows.*"

86400 Seconds

Imagine there is a bank account that credits your account

each morning with $86,400. It carries over no balance from day to day.

Every evening the bank deletes whatever part of the balance you failed to use during the day. What would you do? Draw out every cent, of course.

Each of us has such a bank. Its name is TIME.

Every morning, it credits you with 86,400 seconds.

Every night it writes off as lost, whatever of this you have failed to invest to a good purpose.

It carries over no balance. It allows no overdraft. Each day it opens a new account for you. Each night it burns the remains of the day.

If you fail to use the day's deposits, the loss is yours. There is no drawing against "tomorrow."

You must live in the present on today's deposits. Invest it so as to get from it the utmost in health, happiness, and success!

So, what is your intention? And remember, take some time to say thank you to our merciful God who gave you this day, filled with options and opportunities.

In the end, time is the true currency of life. Not money. Don't ever forget that.

An ancient Sanskrit poem says,

Look to this day
for it is life
the very life of life.
In its brief course lie all
the realities and truths of existence
the joy of growth
the splendor of action

the glory of power.
For yesterday is but a memory
And tomorrow is only a vision.
But today well lived
makes every yesterday a memory of happiness
and every tomorrow a vision of hope.
Look well, therefore, to this day.

Chapter 18: How to Communicate with Your Teenager

Years ago, I saw a sign posted on a wall, and the message has stuck with me since then. The sign read: "*There are only two lasting bequests we can hope to leave our children. One of these is roots; the other, wings.*" Hodding Carter

Understanding our teens, and connecting with them, and really communicating with them, is daunting. We desperately want to continue the unconditional love that existed when they were little; when they were willing to cuddle and snuggle with us; when they needed us to feed them and dress them, and fasten them into their car seats, and read and sing to them at night.

But instead of the sweet, bright little faces you saw in them growing up, and instead of the cheerful voices you heard when they greeted you, you see sullen expressions; eyes roll when you speak. You hear doors slam, see moods that are mercurial, and watch your beloved children constantly escaping to their rooms or their friends' houses to avoid you. You can't get a word in edgewise when their eyes are glued to their phones or their video games. Trying to address problems and disciplinary matters is like trying to put out a forest fire with water from a Dixie cup.

Painful, isn't it? SO painful. So heartbreaking, to see the transformation take place. But it doesn't have to be that way. And, if it is that way now, it doesn't have to stay that way. I'm here to help you make peace with your teen and move forward together in a relationship that is mutually loving and joyful.

Let's start by playing a word game. When I say a word, think of a picture of that word.

Ready? Here's the first word: TRUNK. Got your picture? OK.

Next word: TALE (or TAIL).

Next word: FAN

and last word: BLIND

Next part of the game is to think of words that sound similar to the word I give you. It can rhyme, or it can have the same sounds. For example, our twin granddaughters call a napkin a mapkin. You can create a word that sounds like the word I give you, and it doesn't have to make sense.

Ready?

SPEAR

Next word: TUSK

and last word: EAR

Thanks for playing that little game. Now I'll go over the words I gave you, and explain how it all connects with your unhappy, rebellious teenager.

When I said "TRUNK," what is the picture that came to

your mind? A large suitcase, like you see loaded into the carriage on Downton Abbey? Or maybe the trunk of a large tree? Or did another picture come to mind? What about the word TALE? Did you think of a story? Did you think of a fairy tale, or a horse tail, or a mouse tail, or a private investigator tailing a suspicious character?

When I said FAN, did you think of the rotating blades in your ceiling; that cool you on warm days? Did you think of an exuberant basketball aficionado, sitting in the stands of the playoffs? Or maybe you thought of a folded semicircle of paper or feathers that could be flipped open and waved to create a breeze for your face.

When I said BLIND, did your plantation shutters come to mind? Or perhaps you thought of someone who has no sight. Or maybe you came up with a pull-down sunshade in your bathroom; or a screen for keeping the sun out of your eyes in the car.

When we got to the second part of the game, with words that *sound* like the words I wrote, I am interested to know what you came up with. Since it's highly unlikely that I will hear your response, I'm going to guess at some of them. This all fits in the game.

When I said the word SPEAR, did you think of a sphere? Or a sneer? Or even something like a cheer? No wrong answers, by the way! What about the word TUSK? Did you come up with musk? or dusk? When I said EAR, did you think of here? Or tear? or near?

The point of the game is that words create visual triggers, that may or may not be the intended picture. So when I say to you, "That trunk needs to be moved," it will have a different meaning if we are in the house and I'm pointing to a large piece of luggage, or if we are standing in a gardening center and a tree is in the way.

When we talk with teenagers, we are each communicating with a different frame of reference, and it can be very easy to misunderstand each other. Even being raised in the same home, your children speak a different language from yours, based on their contextual meanings of words, and so you are going to have to take that into account when you try to understand them.

Say for example, you greet someone at the airport who has never been to the United States before. They come from some country that doesn't speak English, and you are trying to ask them things like "what would you like to eat?" or "where would you like me to take you?" Or if you see that they are in danger because they don't come from a place that has a gas stove and they don't know how to use it, how do you warn them?

With a teenager you are going to have to think about communicating with a different kind of language. You don't want to speak like they do, thinking that will put you on a level communication field. That will just be offensive to them, and it will kind of backfire on you. But if you can allow yourself to listen, really listen to them, and wait to have an emotional reaction to what they are saying, you'll make progress. I promise. Just be prepared for a LOT of emotion, because that's all part of what teenagers are experiencing, and they don't know what to do with it.

Sometimes as parents we get into a fearful mode, perhaps thinking this child that we have loved and raised and had so much fun with is suddenly a creature from the Black Lagoon, and we can no longer enjoy them. Suddenly they are doing things that don't make a lot of sense or saying things that don't seem very kind or respectful, and suddenly their friends are WAY more important than their family.

How do you deal with that kind of interaction? Or noninteraction, as the case may be! Sometimes they withdraw from the family, as if they are embarrassed to be related to you. They don't want to eat with everyone. They would rather eat in their room. And chores? Heaven help you if you want them to do their share of chores. Get ready for the eye rolls and the heavy sighs.

What happened to this delightful person? Somewhere inside, the real kid is in there, and if you can figure out the magic words, maybe he or she will come out. At least you hope so!

Well, let's get to the bottom of this.

Misunderstanding can lead to confusion, which can lead to judgment, which can lead to contention that can cause pain and withdrawal from the relationship.

In raising teenagers, is it extremely important to keep safe lines of communication open . . . at all times. As parents, we have to be SO careful not to jump to conclusions that can sever that tenuous bond.

This poem depicts what happens when people make decisions based on different points of reference.:

The Blind Men and the Elephant
by John Godfrey Saxe

It was six men of Indostan, to learning much inclined,
who went to see the elephant (Though all of them were blind),
that each by observation, might satisfy his mind.
The first approached the elephant, and, happening to fall,
against his broad and sturdy side, at once began to bawl:
"God bless me! but the elephant, is nothing but a wall!"
The second feeling of the tusk, cried: "Ho! what have we here,
so very round and smooth and sharp? To me tis mighty clear,
this wonder of an elephant, is very like a spear!"
The third approached the animal, and, happening to take,
the squirming trunk within his hands, "I see," quoth he,
the elephant is very like a snake!"
The fourth reached out his eager hand, and felt about the knee:
"What most this wondrous beast is like, is mighty plain," quoth he;
"Tis clear enough the elephant is very like a tree."
The fifth, who chanced to touch the ear, Said; "E'en the blindest man
can tell what this resembles most; Deny the fact who can,
This marvel of an elephant, is very like a fan!"
The sixth no sooner had begun, about the beast to grope,
then, seizing on the swinging tail, that fell within his scope,
"I see," quothe he, "the elephant is very like a rope!"
And so these men of Indostan, disputed loud and long,
each in his own opinion, exceeding stiff and strong,
Though each was partly in the right, and all were in the wrong!

So, oft in theologic wars, the disputants, I ween,
tread on in utter ignorance, of what each other mean,
and prate about the elephant, not one of them has seen!

In chapter 5, I promised to teach you about Teenspeak. I spoke with you about Childspeak, and how little ones are just beginning to learn what words mean. We learned about how to calm a tantrum in a small child.

There are some significant similarities in our teenagers' experiences, what they are going through, and their inability to adequately address the oceans of emotions they are feeling. Suddenly their bodies are changing. They have to be socially savvy when they are barely recognizing that they need to shower more often and wear deodorant. They are growing, sometimes at such a rapid pace that their muscles can't keep up and they are gawky and uncoordinated.

We all mature at different levels over different timelines and with different outcomes. So while one teen is clumsy, awkward, and socially inept, another one can seem to be confident, graceful, and attractive. Some struggle with growing up, and others seem to just glide into competency without a challenge.

Teens' minds are exploding with SO much information! They have their regular classroom assignments and exams. They are becoming aware of political, social, and sexual trends. They are no longer spending their days in the safety of home. If they go to public school, they face threats and bullying and—sometimes this is the worst issue—not fitting in; not finding a tribe that welcomes them as they are.

So let's talk about the different ways you can learn "teenspeak" and effectively and lovingly communicate with your teens.

It is of tantamount importance that you as their parents maintain a safe haven for them at home and with you. If your home can be a safe haven for their friends as well, so much the better. One of my clients asked me years ago how she could help her son feel more happy with his schoolmates. They lived close to the school, and the kids had the option to come home for lunch. I suggested she feed his friends and welcome kids to their house. Years later, she told me that was the best counsel she had ever had about helping her teenager. In making their home a safe and welcoming environment, she created a space for her son to have friends over, and she had control over the environment. It was a win-win.

That option is not available to everyone, but creating a safe haven in your own space is possible.

The second thing to master when communicating with your teens is the skill of listening. Remember, they are speaking a different language. Words for them have different meanings. They are experiencing emotions that they have no words for. And sometimes, the words they hear at school don't much fit with what is ok at home. Get ready for that. Again, no emotion. It's all in how you listen and how you respond. Maybe they think you're weird and behind the times. But that's ok. They are entitled to think that. You can love them anyway. Maybe they are not doing what you approve of. That's ok too. You love them anyway, and you are going to listen to them and learn how to hear what they are saying.

They are far more important than things. They are far more important than *your* ego.

Patience, and humor will get you a lot farther than you could go by responding with emotion. Remember my model, S-T-R-E-A-M? Your teen is Seeing something, Thinking about it, having a Response, attaching Emotions, taking Action, and then Manifesting results, just as you are. But the sight, thoughts, and responses are triggering different emotions, actions and manifestations than yours would because you have a different frame of reference. Your experiences and way of viewing things are different from theirs.

By the way, this same principle and method for dealing with miscommunication works with a spouse, a neighbor, and even a small child.

My author friend Joni Hilton wrote a great article about communicating and gave me permission to share some of her excellent tips. Here's one, which I am adding as Number Four on your tips for connecting:

"What if your teenager accuses you of being a horrible person who's totally unfair? Try saying, "Wait a sec'. So you think the rules are not fair in this situation. You're angry. Talk to me about that." This doesn't mean you agree with their opinion, just that you're hearing them out.

Her method of listening includes a very important component: making sure you understand by rephrasing. Joni continues:

Buy time. I'm serious. When someone says something that triggers an angry response, start by saying, "I'm so glad you asked that."

Someone says—or asks—something offensive to you. Don't address it immediately. Say a line like the one above, or some variation: That's an interesting question. You're giving me food for thought. I think I have the right response to that. Or even just, I need a moment to collect my thoughts.

This simple purchase of a couple of seconds can make a world of difference. As your mouth is forming just a few short words, your brain will be racing to formulate a response that's thoughtful, respectful, intelligent, and kind.

You can still stand your ground, but without offending back and escalating a disagreement. After uttering that short line you can take a breath, and I guarantee the next words from your mouth will be less flammable than if you had given a knee-jerk response.

Have you ever noticed how fast your brain thinks when you say, "Well..." or "Umm..." and that's just one word! We do it all the time to help us be more diplomatic or to think for a second. And now, with your practiced sentence at the ready, you can avoid jumping into the fight and making matters even worse."

Other phrases that Joni uses are:

"Now that is an interesting perspective. Tell me why you feel that way."

She says,

Maybe my brain needs even more time to work. Usually I'm dumbfounded by sudden rude comments, only much later thinking of the clever comeback.

So I've practiced and can now say, "I'm so glad you asked that. It tells me you've given this some thought, and I'm also glad you feel you can be open with me." Already you are disarming them a bit. Remember how great it felt in school when you raised your hand and a teacher or a professor said, "Good question!" Right away you felt a little surge of confidence. We never outgrow the appreciation of a sincere compliment. It gives just a hint of "we're on the same team; let's work toward a solution or at least a compromise, here."

But a longer response like the multi-sentence one above gives you even more time to react calmly, without a counteraccusation or an emotional outburst of some kind....

Responding with gentleness works!"

Understand them. Although they may look like an adult, and sometimes act like one, usually their brains have not developed at the same rate as their body.

Many teens are wrestling with what is called verbal pragmatics.

Pragmatic language refers to the social language skills that we use in our daily interactions with others. This includes what we say, how we say it, our nonverbal communication (eye contact, facial expressions, body language, etc.) and how appropriate our interactions are in a given situation.

When a brain is developing, or when there has been an insult or a trauma associated with the head, the brain needs time to heal or develop properly. You may know someone who has had a stroke or an accident, and those who know that person the best will tell you, *"She hasn't been the same since the accident."* When their personality changes, or they don't speak the same way, they are unable to synthesize appropriate responses for appropriate situations. Sometimes it affects the ability to empathize; sometimes it affects the ability to assess what would or would not be appropriate in a social setting. So when your teenager acts like a goofball, or blows up at the slightest provocation, or says something inappropriate in front of your friends, it's an indication that they have under-developed social language skills, or verbal pragmatics.

By the way, this can also be exacerbated with stress or issues that are disturbing to them. Again, if you have created a safe haven, it will be much easier to help.

So there you have it: five tips for connecting in a loving way with your teens. Now let's focus on some of the absolutely delightful ways you can enjoy this time with them:

They can be really funny! They can come up with jokes and quips that are spot on. They can mimic political figures or movie stars; they can quote funny phrases from movies. In short, they can entertain you. And sometimes they can think you are pretty funny.

They have interesting thoughts, and it's fun to discuss things that are meaningful. You can reason with them.

They can entertain, earn money, dress, feed, and drive . . . all by themselves.

They are willing to try new things and experience adventures.

They are tech savvy and can help you when you can't figure out how to do things.

They will tell you the truth about how you look. What's more, they will help you look better. Maybe even help you be cool.

They're not a mini me anymore. They are becoming their own person.

You can start to see beautiful ways that their personality is developing. They surprise you with their insights, their thoughtfulness, their compassion, and service. They will surprise you with the fruits of your labor and effort in raising them.

They still love to play! They keep you young. And they make awesome babysitters.

They can be there for you if you have a rough day. And if they can't be there for you, they can fend for themselves for a while.

They are curious. They want to understand politics, climate, the world, the universe, and life. And they question things. They want to save the planet. They realize they can make a difference.

They know now that parents are not perfect. They hold you to a higher standard. They encourage you to get in shape.

They are not boring. They know the lyrics to every song.

They have ideas and enthusiasm about the future. They are resilient.

They still need you. They can be your best friend. They can be strong, but very fragile. They teach you, just like when they were little, about the meaning of unconditional love.

Chapter 19: Infinite Worth . .
. and Worthiness

I am looking at the sun just coming up over the mountain.

Years ago our family decided to climb a trail up a mountain. It was a long trail, up some pretty difficult rocky areas, with several dangerous potential falls. It was not a trip for little ones. It demanded our best physical effort, and several of us (okay, me) needed to stop and rest whenever that was an option.

For some insane reason, we carried a watermelon with us. Our original thought had been that the watermelon would provide us with a delicious reward at the end of our journey. But really—what kind of craziness caused us to think it would be fun to carry a huge, heavy watermelon up a mountain? In retrospect, it seemed ridiculous. I laugh about it now, thinking of how we started out, with each member of the family carrying the watermelon for a ways until passing it off to someone else.

For a time, the person carrying the melon was quite proud of their prowess, declaring audibly how buff they were and how far they could carry it. Later, the pass-offs were done discreetly, in muffled silence, when the melon carrier had literally exhausted himself or herself and needed someone to take over. Eventually even I had a turn.

Step after labored step, up, and up and up and up. Muscles began to tire, started to shake. Breathing became ragged and difficult. Conversation slowed to the barest essentials needed to communicate.

Gone were the laughing, silly comments along the way. We became focused on one thing—getting there. Not having been to our destination before, we kept wondering which turn would reveal the vistas we had been promised. We kept hoping the next one would be it. But alas, it was not. More muscle work, muscles aching now. More pauses to catch our breath. And then there was the watermelon. . . .

Suddenly, incredibly, we arrived at the top. The sun was shining. The sky was brilliant blue. From our vantage point we gazed over incredible, vibrant fields of flowers and jewel-like lakes below. Our view was a fabulous mosaic of colors, of sounds of birds singing, and we felt blissful peace, cool breezes, and inner triumph. We had made it! And then there was the watermelon. . . .

Yes! We had made it, carrying the watermelon all the way. We smashed it against some rocks and dug our hands into the ripe melon, plucking out chunks of juicy, cool sweetness, savoring a kind of primal sense of joy and pleasure at our treat. We cleaned the melon out, wiping our sticky hands on our jeans, and began the descent, feeling renewed and victorious.

As I share this experience, it is just starting to be light, and the first birds of the morning are chirping outside. It is yet dark, but they are singing in anticipation of the light to come. They bring back my memories of that long, dusty, rugged, grueling hike, and the joy that came at the top.

Lately, my thoughts have turned to life and the burdens that come along with it. So many of us struggle with day-to-day challenges or sense of our own personal worth. I have thought of many things I could compare challenges to, such as sculpting a masterpiece out of stone or concocting a gourmet meal for a crowd of 1,000 with no recipe to go by. There are many applicable analogies, but for some reason, the watermelon story came to mind. I decided to tie my philosophical concepts of life and my watermelon story to another concept about our worth and our worthiness.

We could have given up midway up the mountain. We could have sat down on some outcroppings of rock, stared at the trail ahead, and decided that we had made it far enough and we would eat our watermelon and go back. We could have left the watermelon somewhere and picked it up and eaten it on the way back. We could have left those who were lagging behind and gone on ahead with those who were more physically fit. We could have given up entirely and gone home, pretending that we had made it to the top.

But no, we really couldn't. There was something to be learned in the pain, struggle, and empty, labored footfalls of the climb. That something—that amazing discovery—was the gift that came only with our mutual commitment to complete the climb and to do it together. Once we got our "second wind," we began to enjoy the climb. Then, and only then, came the rewarding vistas, the sense of peace and accomplishment. Then, and only then, was the celebratory feast worthy of the effort.

One of the lessons we learned on our hike was that we had to share the burden. Much as each of the boys (and the girls) wanted to prove their invincibility, no one of us could carry the load the whole time. As we became more united and more committed in our journey to the top, we became more sensitive to the melon carriers. Were they keeping up? How were they breathing? Were they stumbling? Were they discouraged? When would it be my turn to carry the load?

Later, my sister and I were talking and she made a comment to me that stuck: "People that try to sidestep adversity miss out on great things." We forget—or maybe we never know—that the joy comes after the commitment and the labored perseverance, even when the climb is demanding more of us than we know we have. Even when the burden is one of great grief or sorrow that overwhelms us, we can feel tremendous joy in knowing we have successfully borne the burden, until it is time to let it go.

Thomas S. Monson said, *"Life is full of difficulties, some minor and others of a more serious nature. There seems to be an unending supply of challenges for one and all. Our problem is that we often expect instantaneous solutions to such challenges, forgetting that frequently the heavenly virtue of patience is required."*

Sometimes, in our uncharitable self-evaluations, we equate worthiness with our worth, our value. I believe that each of us is precious, both to our heavenly family and to each other.

I think of our climb up that long and demanding mountain. We found that encouragement voiced to each other gave us the energy and focus we needed to take that next step, and the next one, and the next one. Our initial pride at doing the best job carrying the melon, or being buff, or walking the fastest, or excelling to a greater degree than the others faded when the commitment to climb was refocused on the journey together. Competition was relegated to the state of meaningless triviality. Creation and commitment and encouragement overtook any thoughts of another's seeming inferiority.

What if one of us had discouraged another on the climb? What if we had been so focused on ourselves that we failed to notice another's shaking muscles, another's tear-streaked face? What if we had spoken unkindly to each other, distracting their focus, mocking efforts to climb, discouraging motivation, minimizing the sense of accomplishment? The top of the climb would not have been sweet. It would have been tainted with regret. In getting to the top, we would have climbed over the confidence of those with us. Our team would have become fragmented. The value of what we achieved would have been lost. Such a victory is a failure.

Gordon B. Hinckley said, "*None of us will become perfect in a day or a month or a year. We will not accomplish it in a lifetime, but we can begin now, starting with our more obvious weaknesses and gradually converting them to strengths as we go forward with our lives. This quest may be a long one: in fact, it will be lifelong. It may be fraught with many mistakes, with falling down and getting back up again. And it will take much effort. But we must not sell ourselves short. We must make a little extra effort. We would be wise to kneel before our God in sup-*

plication. He will help us. He will bless us. He will comfort and sustain us. He will help us to do more, and be more, than we can ever accomplish or be on our own."

In climbing, and in parenting, and in friendships, and in marriage . . . in fact, in all of our relationships with others, triumphs and victories come through building each other. We can choose to build or diminish. Words and feelings of love and encouragement give life. Words and feelings of judgment and criticism kill. It is as simple and as significant as that.

So what do we do when we discover that we are our own worst critic?

Lisa Hayes said, "*Be careful how you are talking to yourself because you are listening.*" *The inner dialog we have with ourselves is so important to observe. We can change our outcome by creating the messages our soul craves: messages of encouragement, hope, confidence, growth, enthusiasm, joy, love, dreams come true. We are, after all, mere infants in terms of understanding all there is about life and our purpose here. It's like trying to navigate a narrow path up a mountain, not knowing what lies ahead.*

Thankfully, God has given us an incredible gift: the ability to create our desired outcome. It may not come immediately, and it may not be easy. We may realize that what was initially so very important to us turns out to be not important at all. We learn that our relationships are what bring the greatest riches, the most satisfying success.

If you find yourself in a self-critical slump, take some time to meditate and focus on five things you are grateful for. Write them down and FEEL the gratitude. When you have done that, if you're still wrestling with your self-sabotage, write down five more, and keep at it until you start to observe everything around you—even your burdens—with gratitude.

Where would you be if you had not kept trying to get up and walk as a baby? What if you had quit with your first feeble effort to balance on a bicycle? What if you judged everyone around you as harshly as you judge yourself? If you've messed up with exercise or diet or any number of other commitments you planned on keeping, each new minute, every new hour, and every new day brings you a chance to turn that around. Ninmar said, "*Stop beating yourself up. You are a work in progress; which means you get there a little at a time, not all at once. Put down that bat and pick up a feather, give yourself a break.*"

If you had a friend who spoke to you the way that you sometimes speak to yourself, how long would you allow that person to be your friend?

A meme that caught my eye read, "*Embrace your humanity and frailty, then figure out how to heal and move on. Be kind to yourself. Forgive yourself. Be OK with being human and being hurt. We have all been there. You think the pain will destroy you, so you minimize it. But if you surrender to it, and walk through it, there are beautiful things on the other side.*"

My wonderful husband is a medical doctor who has seen many diseases that have their roots in unresolved emotional issues. In his lectures, he frequently says, "*We are supposed to walk through the valley of the shadow of death, not pitch a tent and camp there.*"

Release the pain.

Let others help you carry your burden. If no one around you is willing or able to do that, give it to God. In fact, first give it to God.

Forgive the mistakes in yourself and others,

Be patient with yourself and others.

Recognize the law of polarity working in your life. Just as the tides come in and go out, the sun rises and sets, a difficult day will be followed by a great day.

Find gratitude in every experience. We are here to learn. And then we are here to patiently teach.

Make time to visualize your very highest and best self. You can do it in pictures and words, and dream all the dreams that are inside you, wanting to manifest!

Indulge in re-creation every time that you find yourself headed in a direction that doesn't serve you. Get away into nature and take paper and pen with you. Sit on a rock by a flowing stream and pray. Re-create the life you want to live in your mind and write it down.

As Rabbi Harold Kushner said, *"If you concentrate on finding whatever is good in every situation, you will discover that your life will suddenly be filled with gratitude, a feeling that nurtures the soul."*

Chapter 20: Rocking the Last Two Months of the Decade

My husband's father passed away, and two and a half months later his mother died. Her funeral was two days ago, and as I think of this, I am caught up in pondering the concept of time. We looked at pictures and videos of them, taken such a relatively short time ago. Five years ago, they were robust and agile, laughing and communicating with family, participating in events and very much involved. Then their abilities began to show marked deterioration. Steps were more hesitant and faltering. Their memories faded. His dad lost the ability to speak. His mother repeated herself several times, often within a few seconds of having said the same thing. It was difficult to observe the change from vibrant alertness and competence to complete dependency upon others' care.

Sad as this is to describe, some magical things happened. I want to share with you some of the insights I have gained, watching them, and watching the process of dying. The reality is that none of us will get out of here alive. We REALLY need to learn what to expect in life, and we have to STOP playing the procrastination game if we want to leave our physical existence without regrets.

We have two months left in this decade as I write this chapter. So how are YOU going to rock these last two months? Or, since this two months has now passed, what are YOU going to do to rock the next two months of your life?

An ancient Sanskrit writing by Kalidasa proclaims this exhortation to the dawn:

Listen to the Exhortation of the Dawn!
Look to this Day!
For it is Life, the very Life of Life.
In its brief course lie all the
Verities and Realities of your Existence.
The Bliss of Growth,
The Glory of Action,
The Splendor of Beauty;
For Yesterday is but a Dream,
And To-morrow is only a Vision;
But To-day well lived makes
Every Yesterday a Dream of Happiness,
And every Tomorrow a Vision of Hope.
Look well therefore to this Day!
Such is the Salutation of the Dawn!

We are spiritual beings, accustomed to eternity. But our reality now is minutes ticking away in a physical body that will someday die. We have the illusion that time is endless, but it ends for us, on this physical plane. So why do we procrastinate all the things we desire to accomplish while we are here?

If you, like me, have had times in your life when you felt like you were stuck—you wanted to move forward, wanted to make a change, wanted to see yourself achieving your dreams, but you couldn't, STOP IT. Stop the hesitation. Stop the excuses. Stop the whining. Stop the self-pity. You, and only you, are in control of your life. If others around you are holding you back, you can make the decision to move forward without their permission. Your mind is free to imagine and create, and you can take yourself to new dimensions of joy and accomplishment by getting yourself up and moving and becoming who you want to be in this, your only life.

If you thought in the past that you could do all of this by yourself, I have a question: how is that going for you? What have you accomplished by yourself, to move you forward toward your goals and dreams, since you first realized you needed to get going?

Look around you. If you are still looking at the same scenarios, the same excuses, the same fears and limitations holding you back, how well has it worked for you to coach yourself?

You need a coach. I need a coach. We all need to coach and help each other.

So let's get on with figuring out how to ROCK these next two months!

Here are twelve ways you can really change your life and charge yourself with an extra boost of energy and achievement. When you have a down day, go back over this list and see where you can recharge to get going again.

1. Do two things at the same time. While you're driving, sing with the kids. When you are peeling and chopping vegetables, put your phone on speaker and make those calls you haven't had time for. Take a walk and listen to a podcast. Fold laundry while you watch a movie. Take "commercial" breaks and have everyone put their stacks away. Carry note cards in your purse or car and jot down a few thank-you notes while you wait in the doctor's office. A key to this tip is to ENJOY it, rather than feel stressed about it. You are giving yourself the gift of extra time. That way you can do more and enjoy it more.

2. **Tackle the tough stuff first.** This is a major trick employed by every productivity expert I have studied. If you walk into your office and immediately start reading and answering emails, you use up the part of the day when your mind is the clearest doing things that don't require a lot of mental effort. Turn it around so you are working smarter, not harder. Save the filing, the emails, the bill paying, and cleaning for later, when your mind has worked hard and needs a break.

3. **Get your groove on.** When you exercise, you feel better and you get more energy. Dance, walk, take a jog around the block, play pickleball or another sport (that's my husband's passion), go swimming and practice walking against the current. Move, move, move. If your work is sedentary, make sure you get up and move around, doing physical work every ten or fifteen minutes.

4. **Give yourself the gift of an extra hour of sleep.** We tried this the other night and it made a HUGE difference in our day. We normally go to sleep at 9:30 to 10:00. But after the funeral and all the events of the weekend, we decided to

hit the hay at 8:20. By the way, we get up at 5:00, so we're not slouches, really! We both slept soundly for nine hours and felt fabulous all day long. So sleep is restorative on SO many levels, from your brain to your bones. Get to bed!

5. Clean up and get organized. This sounds overwhelming, but if you can figure out where things go and PUT and KEEP them there, you will find success in accomplishing more with less time. For example, grab a file and keep your records, addresses, phone number, and photocopies of all your important documents, such as birth certificates, credit card statements, passports, health and car insurance, go in that file. I did this, and it has saved me so much stress and worry. Anytime anybody calls and needs a birth certificate or other documentation it's right there. If you want a great project to help you rock these next two months, this is it. As an added bonus, you can do a tour through your house with your phone and video your contents. You can send a copy to a family member or friend and keep the original in your file. If you ever need proof for insurance, you've got it. I think of all the people whose homes have been destroyed in wildfires, like in California, and what a mess it would be if you had to verify everything that you owned and remember all of that for insurance. This is a great project.

6. Do it. Do it right. And do it right now. Here is a fun tip: figure out how long tasks take you and then play a game with yourself to beat the clock. For example, if you have items in place so you can jot down and stamp and mail a thank-you note, it only takes about four minutes. Once you get the most important tasks out of the way first thing in the morning, you can quickly eliminate the little projects that have been bogging you down.

7. You are your own first priority. Self-care is important so you can be in a healthy place to care for others. So mark out time to be alone by making dates with yourself. Then you can paint that picture or that cabinet. You can write a poem, cuddle up with a blanket and a great book, exercise, meditate, or experiment with a healthy recipe. If you block out time for yourself and label it as a "meeting," or an "appointment," you are not at the mercy of other peoples' schedules, and you have acceptable ways to say no. "I'm sorry, I have a conflict."

8. Reward yourself! (This kind of ties into #7). You can take yourself out to dinner for a meal that tastes good and makes you feel good too. Try scheduling a massage. Have a manicure/ pedicure. Make a list of rewards that are fun and inspiring for you, and then pat yourself on the back while you enjoy your reward.

9. Look at every task with an eye toward its beauty, and feel the thrill of accomplishment before you embark on the task. Now that may sound a little counterintuitive, but you can personalize everything you do, with that little extra touch that says you did it. Everything you do can have a creative edge to it. Sing. Think. Use ideas that inspire you.

10. Once you get caught up, get ahead. This was a zinger for me. Losing two parents-in-law within 10 weeks got me behind. Our four-year-old twin granddaughters walked into the house and said, "Gammie, your house is really messy! But we can help you clean it." They saw stacks of items we had brought from our parents' house that we were trying to find a place for. Had I thought ahead a little better, I could have avoided some of the chaos.

11. "Light"en your load. (Little play on words there!) When there is little or no sunlight, you have to create your own. So lighten your load with light . . . candles, polished mirrors, clean windows. Buy yourself some bright flowers to lift your spirits and improve your productivity.

12. Affirm the joy in every day. A positive mindset allows you to handle stress with optimism. Harness the power of positive thinking, and visualize what you want. Plan your day with the highest of expectations and FEEL the joy of success. Notice a lot of this is the feelings you're experiencing? Every effort you make today puts you that much ahead tomorrow. Today and every day are yours for the delight you choose to find in them!

If you choose daily to focus on each of those twelve tips for making the most of your day, you will start to see a delightful shift begin to take place in your attitude. Blessings and miracles will begin to appear. You will find yourself on a whole new plane of positivity, and more and more of what you desire will come your way.

Grab a pen and paper and jot down your answers to these questions:

How do you describe your satisfaction with your current situation in life? You might want to scale that one a 1-10, with 1 being the lowest and 10 being deliriously happy.

1. What would you like to change?

2. What are two adjectives you would use to describe yourself?

3. What is your current occupation?

4. What other occupations have you had in your life?

5. What is something that you have done that you think perhaps no one else has ever done?

6. Describe one goal in your life that you have achieved so far, for which you would like to be acknowledged.

7. Describe your feelings from accomplishing it.

8. Did your accomplishment provide a benefit for others? If so, how?

9. Evaluate each of these areas in your life from 1-10, with one being the lowest and 10 being the highest satisfaction.

- relationships
- intellectual (where are your thoughts taking you?)
- spiritual
- emotional
- physical

There are many excellent coaches who can help you to understand the thoughts and emotions you are experiencing, and they can help you to improve the lens through which you view the world around you. As a result, your relationships improve and you generally feel happier. I have benefitted from listening to many of these coaching programs, and I honestly can say that you will come out of those coaching programs better than before.

Commit time to work on your goals every day, even for just a short amount of time. Study, plan, and make the necessary changes that lead you to your desired results.

Be willing to stretch outside your Comfort Zone (which is where your Miracle Zone is!), take action, and complete your plans.

Overcome the stumbling blocks that will inevitably appear as you move forward. Allow for the unexpected, the adversity, the additional time you didn't know it would take. But play all-out, full effort, to do what you commit to do.

Learn the most effective habits for high performance, and you will find yourself achieving more, with more free time for family and fun, than ever before as you apply those habits.

Learn how to create the plan for the life style you want to live.

As a result, you will begin to see miracles happening in your life. You will find yourself able to handle frustrations with greater peace and clarity, and you will most likely find your perspective and motivation and income increase.

In addition to that, you can have the relationships you desire, with yourself and with others. You can have experiences that bring you joy. You can accomplish an almost insane amount in very little time if you know and apply the tools and techniques to make that happen.

There are three elements to achieving the life of your dreams:

1. You must know what you want. You must know exactly, in as much detail as possible. And in making that decision of what you want, be VERY thoughtful. Some of the things we covet aren't nearly as important or as meaningful as we might think they are.

2. You must create the path from where you are to the desired result in your mind and on paper.

3. You must begin immediately, with gratitude and focus, to take the steps necessary to accomplish your goal.

Nelson Mandela made famous a quote by Marianne Williamson: "*Our deepest fear is not that we are inadequate. Our deepest fear is that we are powerful beyond measure. It is our light, not our darkness, that most frightens us. We ask ourselves, who am I to be brilliant, gorgeous, talented and fabulous? Actually, who are you not to be? You are a child of God. Your playing small doesn't serve the world. There's nothing enlightened about shrinking so that other people won't feel insecure around you. We are born to make manifest the glory of God that is within us. It is not just in some of us. It's in everyone. And as we let our own light shine, we unconsciously give other people permission to do the same. As we are liberated from our own fear, our presence automatically liberates others.*"

Chapter 21: If You Knew You Could Not Fail

I'm going to do something a little unusual, something I've never done before. I'm going to share a story with you that is semiautobiographical. I added a little kind of weird element to it so the meaning is more obvious. I think you'll get it when you read it. And then I'm going to segue over to some of my insights from my personal studies.

DO NOT DELETE
By Cristie Gardner

Linsley looked with irritation at the message information in her inbox. "DO NOT DELETE!" were the words, all in capital letters, shouting at her from the screen. She hated those emails, promising miracles in four hours if you sent them to ten of your friends, but a scary consequence if you didn't; the ones hinting of incredible wealth if you read them and sent them on and abject poverty if you deleted them. This message was definitely going to stay unread! Linsley had gotten up early so she could steal an hour of precious time before the kids woke up. The backlog of messages on her computer reminded her of undone work, unanswered questions, un-earned income.

She HAD to get to this stuff today! It was driving her nuts, along with the constant press of laundry, groceries, dusting, vacuuming, and tackling all the clutter. It seemed like every night was punctuated with intermittent little noises, calling her from a sound sleep. *"Mom! I just threw up!" "Mom, I had a bad dream." "Mommy! I'm cold!"* And zombie-like, she would stumble out of bed and take care of it, then return to bed, never quite getting back to sleep. Jeff never seemed to hear them. He needed his rest anyway. He was working ten hours a day trying to make enough to pay their expenses.

I gave up corporate high life for all this? she thought, slightly ruefully. She loved the kids, no question. But their constant, time-consuming demands sometimes felt like they were sucking the very life out of her. She sighed. The choice back in college had seemed like the right thing to do. She and Jeff had gone ahead and had the kids, wanting to enjoy them while they still had energy to play with them and be young with them. Jeff's job was satisfying to him, but it wasn't bring-ing in quite enough, and Linsley felt helpless, watching him from the doorway every day as he left for work. She had the ability to earn a nice income, but being a mom was more than full time. It consumed her.

Today was going to be different. She could feel it. With a burst of energy, she had gotten up, despite the fierce desire to climb back under the downy covers and slumber. Padding down the hallway in her nightgown and slippers, she had turned on the computer, and grabbed her glasses.

While the computer was warming up, Linsley had pulled on her fuzzy robe and tied it around her waist. She had gotten everything ready; now she could start doing some of the free-lance work she had arranged. And then there were those words, "*DO NOT DELETE*," staring her in the face.

Linsley looked at the sender's box. It said the message came from "*Mom.*" Now that was odd! Mom wasn't computer savvy. She rubbed her eyes and looked again. Nope. Same sender. Realizing that she might be taking a risk, Linsley decided to open it. I can always delete it quickly and then run a virus scan, she said to herself.

The message came on. It was a video message. Even more odd, since Mom didn't have a camcorder. As it downloaded, Linsley pondered what Mom could have sent, or who on earth would have the name Mom in the send box.

Then the computer indicated the download was ready to open. Linsley clicked on the screen to view the video, then sat, astonished, staring at the cascade of pictures before her. There were Matthew and Stephen, sitting at the tiny picnic table in the backyard, playing with Legos. Laughing at their silly creations, they were holding them up in the air and zooming around with them. Matthew's reddish blond hair and Stephen's light brown glinted in the sunshine. Their little faces reflected their youth. In this video they were about four and five years old. Now they were in their late twenties. Matthew was about to become a father. Stephen was finishing his first year of teaching English at an international school in China.

The screen changed. This time it was David, Joel, and

Joshua, making a tape for Linsley and Jeff. "*This is the story of Joshua's Elf Christmas,*" David announced into the tape recorder. He and Joel had become fascinated with elves when they were seven and five. Joshie had been three and was agreeable to all of their schemes. Sitting together cross-legged, with their knees touching, the three of them were absorbed in their creative venture. Joel had been blond then, Linsley realized. Now a doctor, his dark hair was almost black, and he wore a goatee. He was father to three boys and a girl. David, a web designer, was now father to four, going on five little ones; his oldest was nine years old. And Joshua, a financial planner, had three—two boys and a girl, as well. They had, all of them, married incredible women. Lori, Heather, Melodie, Brittany, and Alina—Linsley could not have asked for better daughters. "In law" meant nothing to her.

Linsley looked again. The screen shifted to scenes of Emilie and Caitlin, playing dress-up in Linsley's wedding dress and some dollar-store high heels. Now the girls were in college, excelling in music and dance and dating up a storm. It shifted to scenes of Nathaniel, the precious youngest son, who had developed an extra sensitivity with two big sisters as his tutors. His zest for learning had made him a sophomore in college and a paralegal at age 17.

The screen showed a cascade of images and events: the trip to the park, the time at the Scouting ranch in Philmont, the laughter at the dinner table, the puns, the hugs, the precious moments that had long ago faded into memory. There they were, all before her, a vast parade. Then it shifted again to scenes of each of the children, learning to crawl and then walk.

Linsley wiped tears from her eyes as she viewed the scenes before her, not wanting them to stop. She had come into this room with the children still young and had watched them all grow up and become adults. She realized that they were all living their lives away from home now.

She felt a sense of intense regret. She had not recognized the value of each moment with her children when they were growing up. The time had flown, and she had wished some of it away. She had cared too much about clutter and not enough about creativity. She had wanted laundry folded more than sheets spread around the furniture, making forts and secret hideaways.

The movies ended and the screen went black. Linsley stood up from the computer and turned around. In front of her was the door to the home office. Behind her she heard words from the computer's speaker. But the voice was her mother's. "*Do not delete these times with your children, wishing they would get along better, or be more diligent in cleaning their rooms, or wanting them to grow up before it is time. Life is so fleeting! Love them, read to them, cuddle them every chance you get. Enjoy every precious moment!*"

Linsley stepped out of the office, her heart full of mixed emotions. She had watched her family grow up before her eyes, and there were things she wished she had done differently. She walked into the kitchen, absently pulled a glass from the cupboard and began to fill it with water from the tap. Just then, she heard a tiny voice behind her. It was

Nathaniel, this time only two years old. *"Mommy! I need a drink of water!"*

Relief washed over her. She turned and hugged him tight. She held the cup to his mouth and let him drink, all the while noticing his warm little body, his tousled hair, his adorable face. Tucking him back under his covers, she went from room to room, gazing at Caitlin, with her beautiful blue eyes shut, and the lid of one eye purple-green. She had fallen a few days ago and had a black eye. Linsley had decorated the other eye with similar colors from her makeup bag, to make them match. Emilie was asleep, still in dress-up clothes. Usually she and Caitie just wore the boys' old T-shirts to bed. They were big enough to be nightgowns.

She went from bed to bed, watching each of the children in their sleep. The older boys were in their teens; David would be graduating from high school soon. But there was still time. She could remember that this was a different season for her life, one that she would always cherish. Money would come and go; they would have joys and sorrows. But they would be together. And they would focus on the joys. And she would remember.

The End.

Of course, the message on the computer is all kind of weird, but I wanted it to seem as if my mother was reminding me, as she often did when she was alive, to enjoy those precious times and not wish them away. And I started thinking about why it is that we postpone life by filling it in with activities that are meaningless or that don't fit in with our overall goals.

Years ago, Earl Nightingale shared a great book that is increasingly difficult to come by now because it's been out of print for a while. I tracked down a copy and it is one of my most treasured books. The book is by Dorothea Brande, and it's called *Wake Up and Live.*

The big message in Wake Up and Live is to live, and work, and envision, as if you could not fail. Sit down with a pen and paper and write down all the things you would be, and do, and have, if you knew you could not fail. The key to all of this is to ENJOY where you are right now, in this present moment, without giving up the dream of what you want for your future. In my story, Lindsley discovered she was wishing away her present, and forgetting to cherish the absolutely priceless gifts she was experiencing every day. She was taking for granted and wishing away the unique and magical elements of parenting.

Now that my children are grown, I can look with a fresh perspective at those memories that are so precious, I can appreciate them for what they were, and I can share my perspective with you so that you savor those moments. They seem to last forever when you are in the middle of being a parent, but they are so fleeting, and before you even know it, you have moved into a different place in life . . . and so have your children.

There are other elements that are part of a life with joy, living with purpose and significance. I think we all know a lot about those elements, but we forget sometimes. When we forget, it's like the world kind of tanks. We can lose our mental and spiritual footing, so to speak, and we can get caught up in a very scary place without a lot of hope and with very few answers. I recently came up out of one of those places. I'll tell you about it in more detail in my next chapter, and I'll tell you how I came out of it. For now, my big takeaway is to understand that depression and lack of footing are all periodic experiences of life. It almost seems that the deeper down we go, and the darker and scarier it seems, the greater our insight, compassion, and wisdom will be on the other side. And be certain of this: by law, what goes down MUST come up. It's all part of the human experience.

So take Linsley's story, and put it into the context of your current situation. And ask yourself these questions:

1. Am I finding things to be grateful for each day?

2. Am I living in the present moment with joy and purpose?

3. Do I have a clear vision about what I want my future self to be, do, and have?

With question one, I have found it extremely helpful to add five things I'm grateful for each day. I write them down in my journal before I write about what is happening in my life. Sometimes just taking time to notice five things for which I'm grateful is enough to help me make an emotional shift toward gratitude. Where a heart is grateful, it's very difficult to have an angry heart.

With question number two, you have to ask yourself, constantly at first, to take notice of what is happening all around you. I remember thinking, "When we graduate from college, we'll be happy." Then we graduated from college and I thought, "When Stan gets into medical school, we'll be happy." Then he was accepted to medical school and I thought, "If we can make it through this first year, we'll be happy." At some point I started to see a theme, and I got the hint. We make our happy times, moments at a time. Living in the present with gratitude is the best way, and the fastest, to find joy on purpose.

As it says in Proverbs 29:18, where there is no vision, the people perish. Absolutely EVERYTHING you do and become is something that you have thought of in your mind to begin with. Take the time to plan out your vision and make note of actions that will help you to get there. Then live into your dream, happy in the now, and grateful beyond measure. If you do not attach emotionally to the future, you will find amazing things begin to come to you.

Chapter 22: Fluent in Love Languages

In ancient Babylonia, Nimrod founded a city called Babylon, or Babel. This was one of the oldest cities in the land of Shinar. Babylon became part of the Assyrian empire, and after the downfall of Assyria, Babylon became the capital city for King Nebuchadnezzar.

Babylon was an enormous and beautiful city, with the Euphrates River running through the middle of it. Gardens and parks filled a large part of this massive city, which according to Herodotus had walls 56 miles in circumference, 335 feet high, and 85 feet wide. The Book of Genesis describes a significant event that took place in Babylon, the construction of a very high tower, designed to reach unto heaven.

I wonder if the people wanted to hear God more clearly? Not unlike today, if we listen to the voice of God within ourselves, our answers are more clear and peaceful. But when we seek the voice of God, complete with answers to our situations, from outside ourselves (such as the Babylonians did in building a tall tower) to give us the answers we want, sometimes the answers we get are confusing and disruptive to our sense of peace. And for me, it raises the question: is the Tower of Babel in ancient times like endlessly searching the internet today?

According to scripture, the Lord "*did there confound the language of all the earth, and from thence did the Lord scatter them abroad upon the face of all of the earth.*" Later, Babylon became a synonym for both Rome and the world, becoming worldly and focused on outward appearance. Instead of being a place of harmony and unity, it became a place of conflict and destruction. Online, if we spend countless hours searching for answers, sometimes we just get a lot more confused about what is real and what isn't.

Although opinion varies, some have concluded that the city Babel and the word *babble,* as in how babies speak unintelligibly, are related. Whatever the relationship between the word *babble* and the Tower of Babel, Babylon and its Tower of Babel are an effective object lesson in what happens when communication breaks down.

I'd like to address communication in all aspects of our relationships, but most particularly in how we express love to each other. All around us, people are speaking and people are hearing, but they are not REALLY listening, and they are not understanding each other. This kind of repressed attempt to connect results in painful suppression of valuable information, necessary to keep a love alive and thriving. Additionally–and this is what is most frightening–when communication breaks down and we are not truly understanding or reading others' expressions of love correctly, we become suspicious of hidden agendas in each other's comments. Inevitably, our hackles rise when we attach our own personal meanings and prejudices to others' words and unique expressions of love.

In *The 7 Habits of Highly Effective People*, Stephen R. Covey likened our listening skills to assuming that our prescription glasses will work for everyone. Covey said, *"Suppose you've been having trouble with your eyes and you decide to see an optometrist for help. After briefly listening to your complaint, he takes off his glasses and hands them to you. "Put these on," he says. "I've worn this pair of glasses for ten years now and they've really helped me. I have an extra pair at home; you can wear these." So you put them on, but it only makes the problem worse. "This is terrible!" you exclaim. "I can't see a thing!" "Well, what's wrong?" he asks. "They work great for me. Try harder." "I am trying," you insist. "Everything is a blur." "Well, what's the matter with you? Think positively." "Okay. I positively can't see a thing." "Boy, are you ungrateful!"* he chides. *"And after all I've done to help you!"*

Covey stresses the importance of making a correct diagnosis before prescribing. And yet, he points out, we hasten to make assumptions and then prescribe, without knowing the whole story. *"Come on, honey, tell me how you feel. I know it's hard, but I'll try to understand." "Oh I don't know, Mom. You'd think it was stupid." "Of course I wouldn't! You can tell me. Honey, no one cares for you as much as I do. I'm only interested in your welfare. What's making you so unhappy?" "Oh, I don't know." "Come on, honey. What is it?" "Well, to tell you the truth, I just don't like school anymore." "What?"* you respond incredulously. *"What do you mean you don't like school? And after all the sacrifices we've made for your education! Education is the foundation of your future. If you'd apply yourself like your older sister does, you'd do better and then you'd like school. Time and time again, we've told you to settle down. You've got the ability, but you just don't apply yourself. Try harder. Get a positive attitude about it."*

Pause.

"Now go ahead. Tell me how you feel."

See how the focus shifted from wanting to understand, to wanting to be understood?—and without paying attention to the root message? The dilemma became all about the listener, who wasn't really listening at all. Unfortunately, we do this all too often in our interactions with each other.

Covey uses this eye-opening story to let us know how important it is to first seek to understand; then to be understood. If you have a copy of this classic book, I strongly suggest rereading it. It's worth a reminder to all of us about the vital importance of listening with empathy.

We tend to be REALLY good at EXPRESSING ourselves, but terrible at listening with empathy and understanding.

Dr. Gary Chapman, a well-known marriage therapist, spent many years counseling couples whose marriages were struggling, when he noticed a theme running throughout the disharmony in couples. One spouse would say something like, *"I feel like he doesn't love me. The other would protest, "I don't know what else to do! I'm doing everything I should be doing."* Recognizing a pattern, Dr. Chapman pored through years of session notes. He asked himself, *"When someone said, 'I feel like my spouse doesn't love me,' what do they actually want?"*

Surprisingly, their answers fell into five categories, revealing a unique approach in how to effectively love another person. The five categories that Dr. Chapman recognized included:

Words of Affirmation

Acts of Service

Receiving Gifts

Quality Time

Physical Touch

Since his discovery, hundreds of thousands of people have benefitted from identifying their own love language and that of their loved ones.

Pulling these ideas together from Dr. Covey and Dr. Chapman, how do we first seek to understand, and then to be understood, in our own unique love language?

How do we create a relationship that is vibrant and happy, nurturing and supportive?

To get to my answer on this key issue, I'm going to tell you about our efforts to communicate when we were in Italy. Both my husband and I are relatively fluent in Spanish. Spanish and Italian are from the same root Latin language and so there are enough similarities in words that we could usually, with verbiage and body language, get across the rudimentary messages or questions we wanted to convey with the Italian people. The messages were usually relatively simple, so we got the basics across in our communication. It usually (and I stress the word usually because it definitely wasn't perfect!) made it possible to figure out what we wanted to know.

But if we try to connect in that way in a marriage, where we are sharing our deepest thoughts and feelings and fears, we have a potential disaster on our hands. We simply do not have the language skills to speak fluent Italian, with all its nuances. In a marriage, and in a family, the possibility of miscommunication would become a certainty. Bottom line, we HAVE to be able to become masters at both conveying and interpreting each other's hearts, especially in a family.

We HAVE to be able to become fluent in all of the love languages, so that we recognize and honor others' attempts to express love to US. If our feeble and ineffective methods of expressing love are rejected, reviled, and dishonored, we destroy the very foundation of the love that brought us together in the first place.

Ian Maclaran, a Scottish minister in the late 1800s, said, *"Be kind, for everyone you meet is fighting a hard battle."* I'm going to tweak that by saying, *"Be kind, for everyone you meet is expressing themself and desperate to be understood."*

Last week, a single girl in her late twenties asked my husband and me a thought-provoking question, which actually triggered the concept for this chapter. She said, *"You have been married 47 years? Is it still a constant effort or do you have everything figured out in your relationship?"* We assured her that the effort to understand and express feelings with each other is ongoing. We also told her that in marriage and all other relationships, the KEY is to assume the very best motives of each other.

I think it is safe to say that the Tower of Babel is all around us today. People are busy shouting their personal perspectives into the air, with everyone so intent on getting THEIR message across, with very few actually listening with the intention to understand. Whether we speak the same language or not, we are not understanding each other. Then the hackles rise and anger explodes in vitriolic accusations and misinterpretations, from the offices of the highest in the land, to the commentators, to the laymen listening to the news, to the comments on Facebook, to how we treat those we live with and love the most.

How much more significant our interactions would be, and how much greater peace we could achieve, if we understood first, and then sought to be understood second. Let's be aware–REALLY aware–of both the love language that we communicate, and what everyone around us is saying. We tack our past experiences of love language onto the meanings that we assign to others' motives.

For example, if your parents never took time for you, constantly looking at their watch, following a rigid schedule without time to unwind and relax, you would have a greater challenge recognizing the love language of quality time. If you were raised with physical abuse, you might have difficulty with the love language of physical touch. If you were raised in a home where every comment had a sarcastic edge to it, you would tend to be suspicious of words of affirmation. You can make progress in your own ability to listen and understand if you take time to evaluate what in your past has brought you to the place where you are today in understanding, honoring, and expressing love.

What languages do you speak? What languages can you interpret? Become a master interpreter, and the world will change around you to reflect a person who honors all languages of love and returns that love unconditionally.

Chapter 23: Ever and Always Grateful

In June of 2019, CNN featured a story by Benjamin Naughton about a high school senior, Leanne Carrasco, and her inspiring choice for a graduation celebration. Leanne elected not to have a big party, with checks and gifts from family. Instead, she threw a pizza party for the homeless. She chose a homeless shelter for women and children in Houston, Texas, to be the recipient of her gift.

Leanne took a month, a bunch of her friends, and donations from generous suppliers, and prepared four hundred hygiene bags for the shelter residents. They treated the homeless to a wonderful party, gifted them with the supplies, and gave them much more than food and a gift bag. They gave them respect. They gave them a hand up, not a handout. And they gave them validation—the knowledge that they are loved, and important. They turned a gloomy, and perhaps frightening, prospect for the future, into one of hope and gratitude. "*I think you should always know you're lucky to have what you have,*" Leanne said. "*Don't take that for granted and continue to give.*"

I wonder why it is that two of the most "giving" times of year come within the darkest days of the year. Perhaps the contrast helps us to remember the value of warmth, of reaching out to another's needs and seeing if we can lift a discouraged heart and make a difference for good. Albert Schweitzer said, *"At times, our own light goes out and is rekindled by a spark from another person. Each of us has cause to think with deep gratitude of those who have lighted the flame within us."*

Our son and daughter-in-law and their two little boys visited us from Singapore recently. One night we had a bonfire in the backyard and toasted marshmallows and made s'mores. I noted with interest that the flames burned brightest in the logs that were burning together. If someone pushed a hot ember to the outside of the fire pit, the ember went from bright red to black within a few minutes. We need closeness—the grasp of a loving hand, the touch of a caring heart, to nurture us when we are down, and to keep us going through discouragement and despair. Belonging is a powerful part of life. When we embrace each other with a warm welcome, affirmation, and belonging, we connect in ways that empower each other and create a marvelous butterfly effect that goes around the world.

Recently I read on Facebook of a friend who had come to the drive-up window to pay, only to discover that the person in the car in front of her had paid for her order. No expectation of a return, just a thoughtful, simple gift of kindness and a delightful expression of thanksgiving for the abundance in her life. My friend then decided to pay for the order in the car behind HER. She wondered if that was a good thing, or if she just felt pressured to do that. What delighted me was reading a comment from yet another friend. Her daughter had worked at a fast-food establishment, and she said there were times when a whole chain of cars would pull up to the window, each paying for the person behind them. What a marvelous idea! And how fun to minister to one another in a quiet way, saying to the unknown person you are serving, *"I see you. I honor you. I value you."*

Ever and always thankful. I find it very difficult to be sad or depressed when I am grateful. A few years ago, I decided to make gratitude a habit by writing five things I am grateful for each day as I write an entry in my journal. That simple exercise has opened my eyes to the countless ways I am blessed. Sometimes my gratitude is more personal, such as feeling thankful for my fingers and toes. Other times I am filled with thankfulness for the sun and its warmth, or the snow and its purity and the fresh look it brings to the world.

Red Grammar wrote the lyrics to a beautiful song, **"Simple Gifts."**

Tis a gift to be simple, tis a gift to be free
Tis a gift to come 'round where we ought to be
And when we are in the place just right
We'll be in the valley of love and delight
When true simplicity is gained
To bow and to bend we won't be ashamed
To turn, to turn t'will be our delight
Till by turning, turning we come 'round right

Reader's Digest shared this story by Scott Macaulay online: "There's Always Room at His Table."

In September of 1985, when I was 24, my folks decided to get divorced. I was taught that to be a good son, I needed to be supportive and loving to each parent and to my siblings. But nobody was talking to anybody.

If you were nice to one parent, the other one would get mad at you. So when October came, I thought, What's going to happen at Thanksgiving? And I just did not like the thought of being home alone—or anywhere alone—on Thanksgiving.

Thanksgiving is not about gifts or fireworks or hoopla. It's a meal around a table where you give thanks for the blessings you have, and you really can't do that by yourself and have much fun.

I decided to put an ad in the local paper: If people thought they would find themselves alone, they could give me a call, and I would make a Thanksgiving dinner. That first year, a few people came, and they had a good time. I was nervous about making a mess out of the food and disappointing people. But the food was OK, and I didn't burn anything.

I've held the dinner every year since. Last Thanksgiving, 84 people showed up. Sometimes they're new to town; sometimes they're recently divorced or widowed. I've had people who were new to the country and didn't speak any English, but they enjoyed my Thanksgiving dinner. I've had poor people, people who come from AA, old people. Also, not counted within that number: I always feed the police. The firefighters and EMTs are in buildings with kitchens and can have their own Thanksgiving dinner among themselves, but the police officers are in their cars, driving around town on call.

Two years ago, a woman with Parkinson's disease came, and

she was not good on her feet. She had been in a nursing home for seven years and had never been out. Somebody told her about the dinner, and she hired an ambulance to bring her, at $200 plus mileage. She had a great time, and she cried when the ambulance returned to get her. She didn't want to go home.

Most of the people who come don't know who I am. They know that there's some skinny guy in the kitchen, but they don't know my name. I think the theme of my life, and everything I do, could be summed up with the name of an old hymn called "Brighten the Corner Where You Are." I hope my legacy will be that I came into the world, I brightened the corner, and then I quietly left the world unnoticed.

This was recorded on October 21, 2010. I wondered now, eight years later, if Scott was still serving his Thanksgiving dinners. I learned a little more about him when I found this article, written by Cathy Free, of *The Washington Post* one year ago, in 2018. I'll share part of that.

Macaulay, a divorced vacuum cleaner repairman, had an idea: What if he took out an ad in his hometown paper, the Melrose Free Press, and invited 12 strangers to join him for Thanksgiving dinner? It seemed like a manageable number to host at the First Baptist Church he attended—and, yeah, it was a little crazy, but it had to be better than being lonely.

"I knew that I couldn't be the only one in this situation," he said. *"There had to be at least a dozen people out there who didn't want to spend Thanksgiving Day alone."*

Actually, more.

Since those 12 strangers gathered around his table for turkey, stuffing and pumpkin pie 33 years ago, Macaulay has made his free feast an annual event, inviting anyone to make a reservation by calling his office phone number that's printed in the paper. He does not own a cellphone or computer. Through the years, he has fed plenty of widows, widowers, homeless people, college kids who can't make it home—even the guest who crawled under the table a few years ago. All are welcome.

In the town of 27,000 about 10 miles northwest of Boston, Macaulay feeds 60 to 100 people every year. When the oven broke at his church one Thanksgiving, he moved the repast to the basement of Melrose's Green Street Baptist Church, which now donates space for the dinner every year.

About a week before Thanksgiving, Macaulay, 57, who owns and lives above Macaulay's House of Vacuum Cleaners, goes grocery shopping and buys everything himself, though he prefers not to say how much it all costs him because "that would take away the spirit of it." Asked again, he said the total exceeds $1,000.

The menu includes four large turkeys, five kinds of pie (pumpkin, apple, mince, cherry and the ever-popular Hershey's frozen sundae pie), sweet potatoes, stuffing, mashed potatoes with gravy, butternut squash, cranberries, fruit cups and rolls with butter. He stores it all in refrigerators at the church until the morning of the feast.

A few days beforehand, he hauls in sofas, recliners, oriental rugs and even a couple of fake fireplaces, and decorates a rec hall to resemble a cozy living room. Candlesticks and cloth napkins are placed on tables, curtains are hung in the windows, and adjoining rooms are set up for guests to relax and get to know one another over appetizers: chips and dip in one room and cheese and crackers in the next.

"This isn't about the food, though," Macaulay said. "It's about having a place to go. Silence is unbearable, especially on Thanksgiving. My goal is always to replicate the feeling of having a nice dinner in somebody's home."

Reservations usually come in at the last minute, he said, "because everyone is hoping for a better offer." After 32 Thanksgivings, Macaulay can laugh about it and never takes offense. He's made dozens of friends and an equal number of memories.

"There was a guy one year who'd just lost his wife," he said. "And after dinner, he put on her old apron and helped me to do the dishes."

Last year, two people showed up with service dogs.

Another year, Macaulay took a plate out to a woman who was living in her car and was too ashamed of her plight to come inside until almost everyone had gone home.

"She came in to get some leftovers," Macaulay recalled. "And she sang 'Amazing Grace' with this incredible voice. What a year that was."

Then there was the time his parents both showed up. Macaulay's mother was dying of breast cancer and wanted to be with family. So did his dad.

"There they were, sitting on the couch together," he said, "holding each other's hand, years after their divorce. I can still see them sitting there. That's a happy memory."

Infants have spent their first Thanksgiving with Macaulay, and more than a few elderly people have sat down for their last.

Some people return year after year to relax with strangers in front of a faux fireplace.

Geoff Shanklin, 65, who lives alone and has attended every dinner, said he watches in admiration each year when Macaulay makes the dinner happen.

"He prepares it all and we bring ourselves," Shanklin said. "He really enjoys passing it on to lonely people in Melrose. For people like me with nowhere to go, Scott is family."

Last year, Loretta Saint-Louis, 66, was feeling down because she couldn't make it to Ohio for her family's annual gathering. Then she spotted Macaulay's newspaper ad.

"I had no idea what I was walking into," she said, "and I was surprised at how fancy and well-done it was. Scott really goes all out. It's extraordinary that he does this, but he sees it as a gift to give to everyone. He really pulls the little community of Melrose together."

Because Thanksgiving wouldn't be Thanksgiving without giving thanks, Macaulay always asks people to write what they're thankful for on a slip of paper and leave their thoughts in a basket. He saves the submissions and reads them throughout the year, long after the table has been cleared and the dishes washed.

The top thing people write about is being thankful for their health.

"Sometimes, they're grateful they no longer have cancer or that they finally found a job or have a place to live," he said. "One year, a guy wrote that he was thankful his son was speaking to him again. That one was a tear-jerker."

Macaulay also has a son, Walter, 22, who helps serve and clean up. He's the designated turkey carver.

Neither father nor son batted an eye a few years ago when Macaulay's ex-wife strolled in with her new husband and offered to play the piano while everyone ate.

And as for the woman a few years ago who hid under the table?

"I don't ask questions," Macaulay said. "She got served the same as anyone."

I love Thanksgiving, because it helps me to focus on what is really important. The scriptures tell us repeatedly to be grateful:

"Rejoice evermore. Pray without ceasing. In every thing give thanks: for this is the will of God in Christ Jesus concerning you" (1 Thessalonians 5:16–18).

"Be careful for nothing; but in every thing by prayer and supplication with thanksgiving let your requests be made known unto God. And the peace of God, which passeth all understanding, shall keep your hearts and minds through Christ Jesus" (Philippians 4:6–7).

"But thanks be to God, which giveth us the victory through our Lord Jesus Christ" (1 Corinthians 15:57).

"I will praise thee, O Lord, with my whole heart;
I will shew forth all thy marvelous works" (Psalm 9:1).

"And let the peace of God rule in your hearts, to the which also ye are called in one body; and be ye thankful" (Colossians 3:15).

Our family has a tradition of Thanksgiving together, and last year nearly all of us went from as far north as Smithfield,

Utah, down to Gilbert, Arizona, to combine our culinary talents and have Thanksgiving with one of our sons' family. The house was jam-packed with people, and we had to eat in the garage because there wasn't enough seating inside. But the love, the laughter, and the fun made it so enticing that half of us decided to make the trip again this year. (Many of our family have commitments every other year with the other side of their family). We bought our tickets early and were so excited to fly out on the Monday before Thanksgiving.

But to our discouragement, weather came in with snow and wind, and our flight was canceled. I was crushed to realize we couldn't book another flight until two days later. The news announced a winter storm warning for the day we were supposed to fly out. We missed a lot of the laughter, a birthday party for a seven-year-old grandlove, my son's amazing tacos and games and hot tubbing.

What do we do when disappointments steal our feelings of gratitude? We refocus on what we are grateful for. That year, we had time to decorate for Christmas before Thanksgiving! I had time to write a message, designed to help each of us remember how much we are grateful for.

James E. Faust said, "*As with all commandments, gratitude is a description of a successful mode of living. The thankful heart opens our eyes to a multitude of blessings that continually surround us.*"

Cicero said, "*Gratitude is not only the greatest of virtues but the parent of all others.*"

And someone anonymously said, "*Gratitude turns what we have into enough.*"

One of our sons began a nonprofit in Africa many years ago. Every year, hundreds of volunteers come and spend two weeks teaching hygiene and sound business principles, installing water systems, building schools, and in general helping the Maasai tribespeople to create a healthier life for themselves and their children. This service is filled with love from both sides, the givers and the recipients. But each time a group comes back to the United States after serving in Africa, their comments echo the same sentiment: The people have basically nothing, yet they are happy and grateful.

We have SO MUCH to be grateful for. It's time to count our blessings, in each and every moment. What a privilege to be alive, and to be able to participate in the beauties of this marvelous planet and its inhabitants.

Chapter 24: All By Myself?

As we headed toward the end of 2019 and looked ahead to having perfect 2020 vision, a lot of us were making resolutions, with our eyes fixed on solving problems and creating a vision of success in reaching our goals. Are you among those who picked up the list from January 2019, if you could find it, and crossed out 2019 and wrote 2020?

I recently watched a chapter of The Great British Baking Show, where for the Showstopper Challenge, the contestants were asked to create a 3D version of their New Year's Resolution in cake. I was stunned by the choices, which granted may have been due to the complexity of depicting difficult goals in cake. One choice was to wear more lipstick; one was to open a restaurant, one was to call Mom more often, and one chose to tailor his own suit. One contestant said, "I don't make resolutions anymore because I don't keep them."

Seriously, how can we move forward with our lives if we stay in the same place?

And if we DO want to make and keep re-solutions, we have to be able to identify what the problems are in the first place.

This chapter is for those of you who are trying to "wing it" through life. I think we all need, as Zig Ziglar said, a *"daily checkup from the neck up to avoid stinkin' thinkin' which ultimately leads to hardening of the attitudes."*

I'm going to make it clear, from the beginning of this chapter, that you (and I) need a coach, a friend, an accountability partner, someone who will motivate and inspire and encourage you to reach your dreams. And we very likely need more than one. You and I need someone to help us gain a clearer vision of what it is we are here for and how to take the steps to get us there. This includes ridding ourselves of the *"stinkin' thinkin"* that Zig referred to, so we can realize that life is all about sharing our experiences and seeing how we can help each other get to our desired destinations.

Having had eight children, I'm acutely aware of the stage where a toddler has to do everything "by self." Invariably, getting dressed "by myself" results in mismatched clothes, arms through leg holes, and short shirt sleeves to wear in the snow. What kind of mental level makes us assume that we can learn, understand, and implement everything without help? Doing things by ourselves puts us in a frame of mind where we can feel, and be, very isolated in our efforts to changes and grow.

If you're one of those who likes to do it "by myself," I'm asking you, is it working? How quickly, and efficiently, are you seeing positive changes taking place in your life?

The best way to hold ourselves accountable is to have someone who can help us to do that. A good coach can take the shame out and the blame out and replace it with intentional change.

Several years ago, our son Josh decided to get into shape and run a half marathon. And just this past year, he made the decision to get into the best shape he had ever been in his life. On both occasions, he fulfilled his goals, with the support and help of coaching. When he and two of his brothers successfully ran the half marathon, he invited our family to a restaurant and bought dinner for all of us. After the dinner was over, he stood up and said, *"Four months ago we decided to run this half marathon. We put an action plan in place. We followed the plan. We didn't follow it exactly. We missed a few opportunities to train. But we still achieved the goal. It was going to happen. It was difficult to do (except for Nathaniel, his youngest brother)."*

"I want this to be a lesson for my life. It was the decision four months ago that made this happen. We completed the race. Four months ago the fact that we would ultimately run the race was no less true than it is today. And it all came down to a decision we made."

"What do we want to do with our lives? Today? This week? This month? This year? In ten years? What we become is what we decide today to become. When the decision is made to accomplish something, it becomes our future reality."

Epictetus said, *"First say to yourself what you would be; and then do what you have to do."*

Leon J. Suenes said, *"Happy are those who dream dreams and are ready to pay the price to make them come true."*

Celine Dion sang *"All By Myself."* I've changed some of the lyrics to more accurately depict what I'm talking about.

When I was young

I never needed anyone
And setting goals was just for fun
Those days are gone
Livin' alone
I think of all the friends I've known
but my perspective hasn't grown.
Nobody's home
All by myself
Don't wanna be
All by myself
Anymore
Hard to be sure
Sometimes I feel so insecure
Achieving dreams seems so obscure
So where's the cure?
All by myself
Don't wanna be
All by myself
Anymore

As you look over your list of goals for this year, and the next, and going forward from there, you will begin to realize that whatever you face—the hardest thing you have to do—someone, somewhere, has done it. A coach can help you find out who, where, and how the nearly impossible was possible. And completed. A good coach will also help you to identify dis-track-tions: the interruptions that are so much easier than buckling down and getting the most important things done first. Distractions get you off track, and a good coach can help you stay on track.

What's next in your life? How are you going to strategize how to get it? What are the exciting possibilities that excite you? What quickens your heart and creates a sense of anticipation and adventure? How do you turn "*what if*" into "*what is?*" Kobi Yamada said, "*The future is sending back good wishes and waiting with open arms.*"

A friend sent me a copy of the book "5," which shares remarkable achievements people made in five years or less. For example, in just under five years, Michelangelo painted the Sistine Chapel. Shakespeare wrote "Hamlet," "Othello," "King Lear," "Macbeth," and five other outstanding classic plays in less than five years. When he was thirty years old, Jeff Bezos lived in a 500-square foot apartment. Five years later his net worth was $10 billion. Anything can happen in five years!

So many clients regale me with the fear that they are starting too late; if they go to graduate school at this age (whatever the age it doesn't really matter), they will be five years older when they finish. But how old will you be in five years if you DON'T take the plunge and go for your dream?

Henry David Thoreau said, "*If you have built castles in the air, your work need not be lost; that is where they should be. Now put foundations under them.*"

Years ago I read a book by the inspirational author Norman Vincent Peale, called "Imaging." In the preface, Dr. Peale says, "*The concept is a form of mental activity [that] consists of vividly picturing, in your conscious mind, a desired goal or objective, and holding that image until it sinks into your unconscious mind, where it releases great untapped energies. It works best when it is combined with a strong religious faith, backed by prayer and the seemingly illogical technique of giving thanks for benefits before they are received. When the imaging concept is applied steadily and systematically, it solves problems, strengthens personalities, improves health, and greatly enhances the chances for success in any kind of endeavor."* Mark 11:24 confirms the divine concept of imaging things in advance. *"What things soever ye desire, when ye pray, believe that ye receive them, and ye shall have them."*

Let's break this down, so you can really think about what you want your life to look like in five years. I promise you will be surprised at how quickly you will be able to achieve your goal, once it is firmly established in your mind. I'm going to list twelve areas for you to create the image of what you want clearly. Write it down, in your own handwriting. You can add others, of course, that fit your need:

1. Family
2. Career
3. Health
4. Finances
5. Education
6. Recreation
7. Charitable Giving
8. Adventure
9. Travel
10. Romance
11. Relationships
12. Spiritual

"Time is the stuff life is made of." Benjamin Franklin set a

year's worth of goals, with 13 areas where he wanted to improve. Each month he focused on one quality to improve. By the end of the year, he had up-leveled his performance and was satisfied with his personal progress. Franklin set a marvelous example for all of us with his "can-do," fearless approach to problem-solving. He wrote, "*To love life is to love time. Time is the stuff life is made of.*" And over the course of a year, he changed his life, month by month, in the areas of Temperance, Silence, Order, Resolution, Frugality, Industry, Sincerity, Justice, Moderation, Cleanliness, Tranquility, Chastity, and Humility.

Where do you want to be in one year? What about in five years? What is holding you back? Get a coach! Identify and set your course for success. Gift yourself with a new year, and a new you.

Shel Silverstein wrote: "*Listen to the MUSTN'TS, child, listen to the DON'TS–listen to the SHOULDN'TS, the IMPOSSIBLES, the WON'TS–listen to the NEVER HAVES. Then listen close to me–anything can happen, child. ANYTHING can be.*"

What's that magical "anything" for you? Get going and make it happen!

"You gotta have a dream. If you don't have a dream, how you gonna have a dream come true?"

Chapter 25: Celebrating With Clarity

Recently I returned from an absolutely awesome cruise with like-minded women who wanted to mastermind together about ways to build their brands and their businesses. The meetings were wonderful, we all made new and great friends, and the experiences on the cruise were memorable and, in some cases, life-changing.

Coming back was more of a challenge than I had anticipated. I had really missed my husband and family! But whenever I return from a trip, there is unpacking to do, laundry and mail to catch up on, and allowing my body to settle back into a routine. I had noticed similar issues with grieving when loved ones passed away recently. The simple, ordinary chores pile up, while our brains and spirits struggle with finding normal again. We have kept unusual schedules, faced new experiences, and changed the routine momentum we are accustomed to. And, in my case, Christmas was just ahead.

Checking through my waiting stacks of mail and emails, I learned of a program that sounded really intriguing, available for a short time for free, after which I would be charged on a monthly basis. I signed up, began the course, and sent a link to a client of mine who I thought would be interested.

But here's where it all got a little bit interesting, and I'm still working on figuring out all of the lessons I can learn from this.

The most important message I can leave with you in this chapter is to create a life with clarity, having a clear picture in your mind and on paper about what it is you want. If you are not absolutely clear on your desired end results, you will be tempted to take every class, sign up for every free course, buy every program. Some call this the "shiny object syndrome." We keep looking for the solution to the problem, instead of—and believe me this is much more difficult—envisioning and clarifying what our desired end result looks like.

Then, applying that to holidays or other busy seasons, we can come up against a cluttered schedule that does not feed our souls. We hang onto the illusion that our peace depends on organization because a well-ordered life (we falsely believe) is a safe one. In reality, a rigidly structured life leaves no room for creativity, for spontaneity, and for connecting in a deep and personal way.

We can become somewhat frantic with gift giving, and spend more than we need or want to on presents that only add to the confusion after the season. It is wise to approach our sacred celebrations in ways that have meaning, significance, and clarity for us. A Christmas or a Chanukah or other sacred occasion, celebrated with clarity, makes sense to me. On those occasions when my intentions have been clear and my actions congruent, I have used my time to create a treasured memory of precious time with loved ones, serving those less fortunate, and finding meaning, purpose, and joy.

We need the same type of clarity in choosing what we surround ourselves with. Folks from the Depression-era often found themselves fettered with "stuff," because they had been without. Things became a security blanket. When we cleaned out my father's home, and then the home my parents-in-law built and lived in for sixty years, we were taken aback by the quantity of *stuff*. Several sets of silverware, closets stuffed with outdated clothes, files dating back thirty years that had never been purged.

I found it fascinating, as I visited with a client, that she was describing what she wanted to find in her quest to seek meaning and significance with her gifts and talents. "*I just want to find clarity,*" she said. There was the word *clarity* again.

I believe those "coincidences" are little nudges from the Divine to move forward when the promptings come. So let's talk about how to celebrate with clarity.

In a Facebook group, a couple was asking how to deal with parents who insist on giving their grandchildren excessive numbers of lavish gifts. The parents themselves have cleared out the excess in their home, and they have made the choice to make memories through service and travel with their children. Their parents, on the other hand, feel that the only way to express their love to their grandchildren is through physical presents. Thoughtful responses suggested kindly informing the parents that their gifts would be appreciated, but they would be donated to people in need. The parents wanted their gifts to include time and love and service, not what money can buy.

What do you want for your sacred celebrations this year? Do you want them to be filled with feasting and music and partying? Do you want them to be times of contemplation, of renewal, of service and becoming? Do you want a blend of both?

And how would you like to deal with the expected gifts for office parties, or neighborhood exchanges? Do you want to spend your time baking cookies or making fudge? Do you long for the chance to cuddle up in a comfy chair with an inspiring book? Do you want to create an experience your family will remember for years? Do you want to connect in a stress-free way? Each of those options is open to you, but they cannot all happen at the same time. And often, when you choose one, you choose to eliminate the others.

Here are some ways to simplify and focus on what you truly want to have happen. The more clear you are on the desired results, the more likely the desired results will happen.

Here are five things you can do this year to stress less and love more this holiday season.

Limit those to-do's.

Ask yourself, "Will this create meaningful memories?" And more importantly, "Will this add to the peace of the season or take away from it?"

Plan ahead.

For me, the biggest thing to help instill calm into the holidays is to get started early on my to-do list. No matter how much you scale back on the to-do's, some tasks (like shopping for family gifts or planning the food for a family gathering) are inevitable. Thankfully, nothing reduces stress and anxiety like early preparation! I aim to finish the bulk of my to-do's by November 30th.

Spend less, do less.

Another big stressor during the holidays is finances. Giving yourself permission to spend less and do less—like skipping the expensive holiday card or dialing down your gift budget—will leave you with more mental and emotional capacity to really soak in the season.

Get the kids on board.

Early in the season, we gather our family and discuss what kind of Christmas we want to have. We talk about the feelings we want to experience and brainstorm ways to get there—without going overboard. Helping your children catch the vision of a simple Christmas will mean more understanding and contentment for everyone.

Keep coming back to your "why."

When the hustle creeps in, try to ground yourself again by remembering why you want the kind of season you want. For some that may be to connect more closely with the Divine; for others it may be to find more time and connection with your family. Keep holding on to that longing—that desire for a slower, more meaningful season—and you'll find it.

When my husband was in medical school, we had NO money to purchase gifts. We went to appliance and furniture stores and asked if they had some big boxes they could give us. We brought the boxes home and put them under the tree. With watercolor markers and scissors, our boys turned the boxes into trains, and cars, and forts, and grocery stores. They played with the boxes for months until the cardboard literally fell apart. It was a joyous, stress-free celebration of clarity.

Surprising statistics from Simply Orderly about being un-organized:

The average person spends 12 days per year looking for things they can't find.

Every day, the average office worker spends 1.5 hours looking for things.

In a recent survey, 55% of consumers stated they would save anywhere from 16 to 60 minutes a day if they were organized.

23% of people pay bills late and have to pay late fees because they are unable to find their bills.

So much time is being wasted every single day by the average person.

To become more organized, you may want to find a day or life planner that works for you, set reminders on your phone, use post-its to remind yourself of upcoming tasks, and so on.

Just as finding ways to simplify your life is an important thing to think about in the new year, so is thinking about the things that are truly important to you. Any time is a good time to reflect on what you want out of life, and it can help you find ways to focus on how you can achieve your goals.

By making a list of your priorities and the things in life that are important to you, you'll be able to simplify your life by eliminating any extra clutter that may be holding you back.

Think about your strengths and weaknesses to understand whether or not multitasking actually helps you save time. It's possible that you can multitask some things, but others need your full one-on-one attention.

For the most part, by being present in the moment and single-tasking, your ability to focus on one thing at a time and fully complete each task in front of you will help you better focus on the ways to simplify your life.

Over the past three years, I have learned to meditate and enjoy the incredible peace and presence it gives me to focus on the breath and the present moment.

Everyone is busy, all the time. If we are not physically trying to get things done, our minds are working out how to accomplish what we want. All of that can be exhausting when we lose focus on what is most important.

So how are you going to make your sacred celebrations meaningful and simple this year? I have found that meditating and praying first thing every morning help. So does keeping a watch on what I eat, and how much water I need to keep my body healthy. These practices are restorative and help us to get centered on what is the most important for our happiness;

In fact, our Joy on Purpose.

As you finish your Christmas or Chanukah or any other sacred celebration preparations, keep these ideas in mind and simplify, simplify, simplify, using your vision of what the end result looks like to decide what to keep, and what to forget about this year.

God bless us, every one!

26

Chapter 26: Finding Meaning and Purpose in Pain

Despite the lights and the laughter and the majesty of sacred and memorable celebrations, many people struggle with challenges at celebratory times of year. For some the challenges are huge, even seemingly insurmountable. This chapter is for those of you who are struggling or know loved ones who struggle, and it is for you that my prayers of hope and comfort reach out with my message. I want you to know, despite how things seem right now, they will get better. Just hang on. Hope and light will come.

Ten years ago at this time of year, my mother was dying of cancer that had spread throughout her body. She was an incredibly gracious lady. The most that she ever took for her pain was an extra strength Tylenol on occasion. At Thanksgiving, she asked my husband, a medical doctor, what was wrong because "she just didn't feel good." As he did a physical exam, he could feel the massive tumor. Tests confirmed his suspicions. She had only a few weeks to live.

With what strength she had, despite the pain, she made a point of calling all her friends. "*I'm dying,*" she said cheerfully, "*and I just wanted to make sure you know how grateful I am for your friendship . . . or your encouragement . . . or your support,*"—whatever feelings she wished to express. She made sure we opened our gifts from her early, so she could see our faces. She had made counted cross-stitch pictures that were stunning, working on them all year to make sure we had a gift of love from her.

At the same time as my mother was dealing with her graduation to God's presence, our son and his wife were in the hospital, awaiting the birth of their baby boy on the 18th of December. At birth he appeared normal, but two of his fingers were fused together and there was a hole in his heart. Tests confirmed our little Robbie had Down syndrome. He would need many surgeries early in his new little life. Our son and his wife faced tremendous challenges, all unknown when this precious little boy was born.

And just twelve days after Robbie's birth, my angel mother passed away.

I remember asking for the soft blanket that another son and his wife had given to Mom early for Christmas. She had passed with the warmth of that soft blue blanket covering her. I wrapped myself up in her blanket and sobbed and sobbed. I missed her so much already—missed her wisdom and humor, her example and listening ear. I had regrets of not making enough time in my schedule to talk to her as often as I could have.

When I wanted to be a support to my son and his wife

with their new little Robbie and their other children, I was almost paralyzed with grief that came in waves, longing for my mother to be with me, longing to be healed from pain.

It didn't happen overnight, and those were some of the most wrenching times of my life, but things got better. Peace came in the moments when I thought of her with love and gratitude. Peace also came with my awareness that I had truly been blessed to have had her in my life. Whether for a short or long time, the gift of her influence and love in my life was profound and everlasting.

Many people struggle with pain. Sometimes the pain is emotional, sometimes it is a pain of regret, and sometimes the pain is physical. Sometimes we find ourselves alone and lonely. Sometimes we deal with loss, whether loss of loved ones or of security, loss of home or friendship, loss of hope. Sometimes, in the middle of winter, the "*most wonderful time of year*" is difficult, and it's challenging to find something wonderful.

Pope Paul VI said, " *All life demands struggle. Those who have everything given to them become lazy, selfish, and insensitive to the real values of life. The very striving and hard work that we so constantly try to avoid is the major building block in the person we are today.*"

Here's my promise to you: things get better. By law, known as the law of polarity, our reverses and struggles can and will eventually shift into joy and prosperity. We gain perspective as we search for meaning to assuage our pain. As Marianne Williamson said, "*Healing is a return to love. Illness and death are often painful lessons in how much we love, but they are lessons nonetheless. Sometimes it takes the knife that emo-*

tionally pierces our heart, to pierce the walls that lie in front of it."

The law of polarity helps us to understand the value of contrast: light vs. dark, night vs. day, sleep vs. awake, joy vs. sorrow. When we feel stuck in a place of pain, we can hold on, knowing that change will happen. When I am feeling pain, I can have faith that things will get better. Helen Keller (whose life was a study in triumphing over pain and difficulty, had this to say: *"Faith is the strength by which a shattered world shall emerge into the light."*

A friend of mine shared on Facebook that her self-describing word is "shatterproof." She has faced numerous challenges with life, marriage, health, and business, but she has declared, and lives by the mantra, that she is "shatterproof." I love that she has exercised the faith to emerge into the light and understands the value of becoming shatterproof.

Giving birth to each of my eight children is a metaphor for this experience. You have to experience the pain, move through the pain, and transcend the pain that engulfs your muscles as your body gives birth. We were taught to call that experience "contractions" instead of labor pains, and there is value in recognizing what is happening in our body as we bring a new little person into the world. But for me, at least, it didn't feel good. It hurt. It hurt a lot, and I would call that pain. At the end, however, was the beautiful experience of a precious new baby to love and care for. I had to move through the pain to get there. The pain was worth it, millions of times over. In fact, the pain became a distant memory as soon as I held my baby in my arms. All too often, we as moms comment on the experience and how it was for us, but I thought about the baby in the womb, going through tremendous challenges to be born! What kind of pain and sorrow is this tiny new being experiencing, after having developed with every need met, floating in a sea of peace and nurturing? Suddenly, they are squeezed and propelled, without being aware of the pain that lies ahead, through the birth canal and into bright light, from a world of quiet, muted sounds and vision. No wonder it takes a baby a little while to smile!

When you go through pain, what is the birth or rebirth that you are experiencing? In my case with my mother's death, I have experienced time and again, precious memories of her wisdom and humor, her patience and support, and I feel that I renew that life and love she lived when I extend it to my children and their children, and others around me. She gave me foundational wisdom to deal with life experiences in a more tranquil way, to understand the significance behind suffering, and to cherish the knowledge that gives me.

Sometimes we have an inkling of what lies ahead, and it creates fear and resistance in our hearts. We would do almost anything to avoid the hurt that we know is coming. I submit to you that the greatest pain is the pain of regret: regret that we did something we should not have done, or we caused great sorrow to another, or we failed to allow ourselves the experience that would have helped us to grow tremendously.

When we have gone through something traumatic and difficult, we want to help others that we can see going through similar experiences. But that's the magic, and the mystery, of life's journey. Each must go through their own struggles themselves. That doesn't mean we do it alone. It means that we give one another strength by their knowing we are beside them, with prayers, empathy, encouragement, and love. My cousin posted this on Facebook:

"When someone is broken, don't try to fix them (you can't). When someone is hurting, don't attempt to take away their pain (you can't). Instead, love them by walking beside them in the hurt (you can). Because sometimes, what people need is simply to know they aren't alone."

I love what Joseph Campbell said, *"Find a place inside where there's joy, and the joy will burn out the pain."*

We feel the greatest pain and hopelessness when we are in isolation. We feel the greatest empowerment when we know that people we love are there for us. When we watch movies about police, we constantly hear the partners tell each other that *"I have your back,"* or *"Watch my six."* Using the old pilot system, where directions correspond to the numbers on a clock, "six" came to mean the back, or coming from the rear.

Caroline Myss said, *"We are not meant to stay wounded. We are supposed to move through our tragedies and challenges and to help each other move through the many painful Chapters of our lives. By remaining stuck in the power of our wounds, we block our own transformation. We overlook the greater gifts inherent in our wounds–the strengths to overcome them and the lessons that we are meant to receive through them. Wounds are the means through which we enter the hearts of other people. They are meant to teach us to become compassionate and wise."*

If you are going through great pain at this time, or any time, of the year, you have tremendous power within you to change all of that. You are a creator. You have the ability to create your reality, to decide what you want and go after it. You can move through the pain and into a place of joy. You must be very specific about what you want, visualizing it in as detailed a way as you can. You do NOT need to worry about HOW it will happen. Just hold on to the vision you see in your desired results. Ben Okri said, "*The most authentic thing about us is our capacity to create, to overcome, to endure, to transform, to love and to be greater than our suffering.*"

I have watched with sorrow as friends post on social media that they are helpless to change whatever crisis they are facing, and pleading for help: money, child care, heavy lifters to move stuff, and so forth, to alleviate their suffering. The whole mindset of needing rescue propels us to victim status, and as victims we deny our incredible and undeniable power to transform our circumstances through our mindset and our actions. That does not mean, of course, that we should ignore pleas for help. But maybe the three most powerful words someone can hear when they struggle are these. "You got this!" With encouragement and hope and friendship, we can find amazing resiliency within ourselves, and have courage to face another day with gratitude in our hearts that we get to HAVE another day!

Barry Neil Kaufman said, "*Gratitude is one of the sweet shortcuts to finding peace of mind and happiness inside. No matter what is going on outside of us, there's always something we could be grateful for.*"

Corrie Ten Boom, who had reason to feel she was a victim if anyone did, is an example of perseverance and gratitude. Imprisoned in the concentration camps, she and her sister were in a barracks infested with fleas that bit and created miserable, itchy welts. They had to have their heads shaved and suffered incredible hardship with illness, cold, and starvation. But because they chose to look for the good, and be grateful, in ALL things, they realized that the guards stayed away from the barracks with the flea infestations, keeping the women housed within safe from predatory abuse. They were also able to read their Bibles without interference from the guards. Corrie's suffering and the insights she gained later gave her the strength and divine courage to forgive one of the most hateful and abusive guards when he came to her, filled with remorse and hope, to request her forgiveness. John Green said, *"Beautiful are those whose brokenness gives birth to transformation and wisdom.*

There's a metaphor for the pain we go through. While we are going through difficult times and circumstances, it almost seems that time has stood still and our suffering is forever. But reality is that pain does not endure forever. If we hold on, the light will come. Marianne Williamson said, *"The greatest gift we can give to a person in pain is to hold in our own minds the thought that there is a light beyond this darkness."*

Hold onto the sure knowledge that this, too, will pass, and you will be stronger and better for your experiences, however painful they may be. I send you light, and love, and hope, and courage, along with the prayer that this and every season may bring you joy, even through pain.

Chapter 27: The Very Best Present

Christmas, Chanukah, Kwanzaa, and many other occasions create opportunities to put aside typical worries and celebrate each other. A lot of us have struggled, to put it mildly, trying all year to find the perfect gift, the one that will leave everyone feeling peaceful, and joyful, and happy you took the time to find the perfect gift for them.

And I found it. I'm going to devote this chapter to tell you how you can create the perfect gift. It will cost you something, but it won't leave you with less money than you had when you started shopping. It won't take much of your time, and I can guarantee it WILL be worthwhile. It is a rare treasure, and yet its value is too often underestimated. It is something that cannot be wrapped because its dimensions are limitless.

And no, I'm not writing about love. I'm also not referring to cute little whimsical thoughts, although those all have meaning and can be valuable in their own way. This gift is the perfect gift for family, spouse, parents, loved ones, friends, and even, yes, even . . . enemies.

The greatest presents are just that. Just like the whole

meaning and significance of the book *Think and Grow Rich* can be found in the title, the best gift can be found in the title of this chapter. The very best present is just that... to be PRE-SENT.

To be present, to listen, to acknowledge "*I see you*," "*I hear you*," "*I honor that you are in my life and I am in yours in this present moment, and you have my full, undivided attention, my total presence.*"

In order to be fully present, we have some work to do. Our work involves focus. It involves attention and self-mastery. Brendon Burchard describes it this way:

"*Self-mastery is full presence. It's joy, it's confidence, it's a positive range of our psychology that makes us have reverence for the moment so now we can dance together.*"

I love the idea of "*the dance together.*" Isn't that what we do, every time we engage another person, friend or foe, known or unknown, in an interaction? From the open smile at the grocery store to the contact on the phone; from the loving caress of a parent on a newborn child's head to the comforting arm around our shoulder at church: we all connect with each other, and each contact builds or diminishes our humanity.

Brendon Burchard continued with these thoughts: "*If you're looking for ways to start the new year off right and create lasting habits, learn how presence changes everything. Life loses magic because we forget to bring the magic and experience the magic intentionally.*"

What does being fully present cost you? Sometimes it costs your ego. Sometimes it costs you your need to be right. Sometimes it costs you feeling that all is fair. Sometimes it costs you humility, or forgiveness, or anger. But I can promise you this: if you can establish the habit to be fully present in your interactions with others, you will experience healing inside you that will transcend any of the stretching and discomfort you feel. The feeling you will have will be one that comes from the spirit within, and it beholds and honors the majesty of the being before you, no matter how weird, how seemingly unlovable, or how small.

C.S. Lewis said, "*It is a serious thing to live in a society of possible gods and goddesses, to remember that the dullest most uninteresting person you can talk to may one day be a creature which, if you saw it now, you would be strongly tempted to worship, or else a horror and a corruption such as you now meet, if at all, only in a nightmare. All day long we are, in some degree helping each other to one or the other of these destinations. It is in the light of these overwhelming possibilities, it is with the awe and the circumspection proper to them, that we should conduct all of our dealings with one another, all friendships, all loves, all play, all politics. There are no ordinary people. You have never talked to a mere mortal. Nations, cultures, arts, civilizations – these are mortal, and their life is to ours as the life of a gnat. But it is immortals whom we joke with, work with, marry, snub, and exploit—immortal horrors or everlasting splendors.*"

Several years ago, I was fascinated to learn of a tradition that exists in many of the Polynesian nations. Although the information is slightly different, depending on where you learn about it, there are sufficient similarities to make this an inspiring personal development quest. I believe in the essence of what this teaches:

In many Polynesian cultures, it is believed that a person's errors (called hara or hala) caused illness. Some believe error angers the gods, others that it attracts malevolent gods, and still others believe the guilt caused by error made one sick. In most cases, however, specific 'untie-error' rites could be performed to atone for such errors and thereby diminish one's accumulation of them.

Among the islands of Vanuatu in the South Pacific, people believe that illness usually is caused by sexual misconduct or anger. The therapy that counters this sickness is confession. The patient, or a family member, may confess. If no one confesses an error, the patient may die. The Vanuatu people believe that secrecy is what gives power to the illness. When the error is confessed, it no longer has power over the person.

Apologizing does not always mean you're wrong and the other person is right. It simply means that you value your relationship more than your ego.

"*Ho'oponopono*" is defined in the Hawaiian Dictionary as:

(a) "*To put to rights; to put in order or shape, correct, revise, adjust, amend, regulate, arrange, rectify, tidy up make orderly or neat, administer, superintend, supervise, manage, edit, work carefully or neatly; to make ready, as canoemen preparing to catch a wave.*"

(b) "*Mental cleansing: family conferences in which relationships were set right (ho'oponopono) through prayer, discussion, confession, repentance, and mutual restitution and forgiveness.*"

Ho'o creates a verb from the noun pono, which is defined as: "*goodness, uprightness, morality, moral qualities, correct or proper procedure, excellence, well-being, prosperity, welfare, benefit, true condition or nature, duty; moral, fitting, proper, righteous, right, upright, just, virtuous, fair, beneficial, successful, in perfect order, accurate, correct, eased, relieved; should, ought, must, necessary."*

Ponopono is defined as *"to put to rights; to put in order or shape, correct, revise, adjust, amend, regulate, arrange, rectify, tidy up, make orderly or neat."*

In the late twentieth century, courts in Hawai'i began to order juvenile and adult offenders to work with an elder who would conduct ho'oponopono for their families, as a form of alternative dispute resolution. The ho'oponopono is conducted in the traditional way, without court interference, with a practitioner picked by the family from a list of court-approved providers.

I believe with all my heart that God is ALWAYS fully present with us; that He hears our prayers. He sees our grieving, our pleading reach for answers. He knows what we have gone through because He gave His only Son, who experienced it all, and stayed present, and gave Himself, the perfect Gift, to each of us. All religions regard Him as a great Teacher, Leader, Rabbi, and Holy Man. I am in awe of His gift to us, and grateful to know that He is present and that we can share our pains and sorrows with Him and He understands. And I also believe that He is present with us each moment, to invite us to increase our spiritual capacity to see others as He sees us.

When we are present with each other, things are put to right. We fill our hearts with lightness, and hope, and forgiveness, and love, and healing.

Focus on giving the present of true presence for everyone who comes within your sphere of influence. Ask God to know how to do that And I know He will show you!

Chapter 28: Creating Your 2020 Vision

We went to Lake Powell with two of our sons and their families, and had a great time riding in the boat, reading, playing in the water, climbing up to the crest of a small rock hill and praying and meditating, and, of course, wake surfing-- or at least in my case and Stan's case, attempting to do so. I won't even try to tell you about my efforts, except to say I ended up being towed back to the houseboat holding onto the knee board. But in Stan's case, he successfully surfed after face planting in the water four times.

About a month later, we were at a family reunion and Stan noticed his visual field had changed. His peripheral vision was gone in the right eye, and he had lost some of the vision field above and below. The ground seemed wavy where it was flat. So he went to an ophthalmologist, who told us to go straight to the hospital. His retina had detached and needed immediate surgery if they were to save his sight in that eye.

Recovery was a miserable experience and took a long time. He couldn't travel to an elevation much different from our home town, couldn't lift much, had to sleep with his face down as much as he could, couldn't sleep on his back. And it was painful. Now we are very grateful that after his recovery, the vision in his right eye is about 20/50.

Fast forward to December. I went on a business cruise with some of my good friends, and we spent one day playing in the water with dolphins. At one point, the dolphins come up behind you and you grab their fins, to be pulled through the water at a really fast speed. They also come up underneath the balls of your feet and lift you up out of the water, in perfect balance, so that you are standing on top of their snouts. What a rush! It was an incredible experience!

When I got back from the cruise, I began to notice changes in MY visual field. There was a slash that looked like lightning in my right eye, and little wavy lines that kind of looked like spider legs. Fearing the worst, we went again to the ophthalmologist. He confirmed that I also had a detachment, only it wasn't the retina. It was the vitreous, which is the gel in the eyeball that attaches to the retina. So although the doctor told me I am at risk for a retinal detachment, I don't have to go through all the misery that Stan did, and as long as I don't do kickboxing or play with dolphins any more, my vision should be fine.

When a person's vision is perfect, eye doctors tell us it is 20/20 vision. When we looked ahead to the year 2020, it seemed like the perfect time to develop a 20/20 vision. Little did we know the challenges we would face, with a pandemic, loss of over 30 million acres and millions of animals and structures and people in wildfires in Australia, murder hornets, earthquakes, swarms of locusts in Africa, riots, California wildfires, hurricanes, tornadoes, floods, "meth-gators," and seemingly countless other weird and scary events.

How many of you make New Year's resolutions? I confess I do. Sometimes all I did in the past was pull out the previous year's list (if I could find it), cross out the year, and rewrite the exact same resolutions for the upcoming year.

RESOLUTION. If you take the word apart, and realize it is a re-solution, you have to be able to identify the problem. And if you keep having the same re-solutions, year after year, how is your vision working for you?

"Where there is no vision, the people perish: but he that keep-eth the law, happy is he." (Proverbs 29:18)

When we have a vision of possibility, an idea that sparks our mind and shows light on solving a problem or reaching a goal, we can feel both excited and depressed at the same time. We are excited because our mind and heart see the possibility, but we are depressed because we don't see the way to get there. When that happens, hold on and keep moving toward your desired end result.

Added to that, things can happen that throw us off. Not just CAN happen; they DO happen. And when they happen, we learn to understand the law of opposition, which can help us to get through the dark times.

Og Mandino said, *"I will love the light for it shows me the way, yet I will endure the darkness for it shows me the stars."*

There are countless laws that govern the way the world operates. I'm not referring to speed limits, or minimum voting age, or income taxes. Those are all laws that people have made to operate in society with less confusion. I'm talking about understanding that there is a law, decreed in heaven before the foundations of this world, upon which all blessings are predicated. And when we obtain any blessings from God, it is by obedience to that law upon which it is predicated. This concept has been discussed for centuries, but we are only at the beginning of harnessing the knowledge of God's laws and using them to progress.

You have heard of the law of attraction. That is just one of an infinite number of laws. And it can be tricky to understand exactly how each law works, but it is a gratifying quest to learn of God's laws and put ourselves to the test.

We are familiar with the law of gravity. We can't ignore that law without consequences. You jump off a cliff, you're going to go down. But we can learn to work WITH the law and use it to our advantage. Sometimes we can combine our knowledge of different laws to achieve what was once thought impossible. For example, if the law of gravity is in effect without exception, an airplane wouldn't be able to get off the ground. But according to a principle of aerodynamics called Bernoulli's Law, fast-moving air is at lower pressure than slow-moving air, so the pressure above the wing is lower than the pressure below, and this creates the lift that powers the plane upward. Thus an airplane can fly, with hundreds of thousands of pounds in passengers, baggage, and fuel, and go through the air at a tremendous rate of speed.

We get one life. When things happen that throw us off, we have to understand that challenges are part of life. How do we do that, when the best-laid plans to keep our resolutions are falling apart? Life gives us circumstances that are difficult, painful, and unplanned. A lot depends on the foundation we use when we are planning our future.

Here are some steps that I recommend for developing a more effective 2020 Vision that will work for you, despite what year it is, and despite the unpredictable challenges you face. You can apply the same steps with your family, health, financial, intellectual, professional, physical, and spiritual goals.

The first step (they all start with the letter "P" to make them easy to remember) is to **PRAY**. Study things out in your mind first, and pray to ask God for guidance. If you pray with real intent, God will give you the answers that you seek.

Second, have a **PURPOSE**. When I write my goals, I try to get to the root purpose of my goal. I do this by writing the goal, then adding the words "so that I can _____ " and fill in the blank, then again adding the words, "so that I can _____, " until I have gotten down to the core purpose of my goal. For example, I want to release 20 pounds, SO THAT I can walk without pain, SO THAT I can take the children hiking, SO THAT I can spend more time with my family and feel increased energy by being healthy.

Third, make a **PLAN**. A goal without a plan is just a wish. Create a bridge of actionable items from where you are to your goal. Jim Rohn said, *"Discipline is the bridge between goals and accomplishment."*

Fourth, **PREPARE**. Use the many and wonderful resources available to you. Other people have insights and experiences to share that will help and guide you. And don't hesitate to explore the inspiration you feel along the way. God is very much in the details of our lives. Together you will accomplish SO much more than you will alone.

Fifth, **PRESS FORWARD**. Recently we were watching a basketball game, and Stan was explaining to me about what it means when there's a *full court press*: a basketball term for a defensive style in which the defense applies pressure to the offensive team the entire length of the court before and after the inbound pass. Pressure may be applied man-to-man, or via a zone press using a zone defense.

So pressing forward means giving it all we've got, using our focus and our vision and our commitment to fuel our action and carry us to the goal. A Note from the Universe said this: *"Persistence isn't about knowing on one door until the dang thing opens. It's about knocking on all the doors. Insist on the destination, not on how you'll get there. Knock, Knock, The Universe."*

There's a lot of significance to knocking on all the doors!

If we are going to take ourselves and our lives to a brand new level in this new decade, we need to tap into divine law and learn to live with the law in ways that unite our power with God's power. When we do that, fearlessly and full of faith, we can tap into energy, knowledge, experience, inspiration, and achievement we only dreamed to be possible.

One hundred years ago, the 1920s were known as the Roaring 20s. You have the ability to decide how each decade will look for you. Depending on your vision and your action, you can have a new version of the Roaring 20s, or you can have the Boring 20s, the Crazy 20s, the Lazy 20s, or something else! It's up to you. I hope you will accept my challenge to make to make your coming year (whatever month it is that you are in!) the beginning of your dreams come true, despite the difficulties. Dare to be who you are. Dare to be the beautiful YOU that God created you to be. Dare to use your gifts. Dare to be strong and courageous. Dare to recognize the strength and beauty you have within. Dare to lead. Dare to speak. Dare to be compassionate. Dare to forgive and move forward. Dare to accept responsibility for where you are and then dare to change it. Dare to be! You have a work that no one else can do, with your unique skills and gifts. You are one of a kind, and you are a wonder! You have the power within you to make miracles happen as you take God's outstretched hand and trust in Him.

Chapter 29: Making Mighty Changes

For many of us, the year we turn thirty is a year of mighty change. We realize how quickly time flies. For most of us, by our late twenties we are moving past the years of getting our education and training in our chosen field of employment, and we are getting settled in our lives and relationships. We begin thinking more seriously about permanence and "what we want to be when we grow up." (Of course, there are also many of us who are still asking that, way past our twenties and thirties!). Maybe the whole concept of what we want to be when we grow up is flawed, because we are constantly growing, constantly becoming.

Sometimes we feel fixed and inflexible when it comes to making changes. And as life continues at what sometimes seems to be a breakneck pace, we sometimes find ourselves seeking more stability and rigidity!

In high school, we learned to make a perfect circle using a compass. Not the magnetic compass you use to tell what direction you are facing. This compass had two legs, one pointed and the other that held a pencil. You stuck the pointed end of the compass onto a spot that was to be the middle of the circle, and then a pivot in the top of the compass allowed the other leg with the pencil to rotate and draw a perfect circle. If you took a straightedge and drew a line through the circle's center, you created a direction that went on forever, an infinite line. If you drew two lines through the middle of the circle, the distance between the lines became greater as the lines extended.

In the same way that the lines from the center point of a circle can extend forever, every time we make a decision, there is a trajectory that extends out beyond our immediate vision, that leads to a result or results that have far-reaching effects.

We make thousands of decisions daily. Each of those decisions intersects with others at one point in our lives and then goes on to lead to results. Years later, we can often trace our results back to the point where we made and executed a decision. Sometimes our results led us to results we can be proud of. Other times we lament over a foolish choice and the painful consequences.

It all goes back to the moment of decision.

Our decision-making process begins with each waking moment, from the time we choose to open our eyes, to whether or not we decided to meditate and pray before we get ready for the day, to the words and tone we choose in speaking to each other, to whether we answer the phone, what we choose to eat, what we choose to do in our more idle moments, to the thoughts we choose to entertain. The list is endless, just as the results are.

Dr. Benjamin E Mays wrote:

I have only just a minute,
Only sixty seconds in it.
Forced upon me, can't refuse it.
Didn't seek it, didn't choose it.
But it's up to me
to use it.
I must suffer if I lose it.
Give account if I abuse it.
Just a tiny little minute,
but eternity is in it.

Take a serious look at your life. What are the results of your life so far? What are you pleased with? Where do you feel you really rocked it? Where did you amaze yourself? Where did you experience victories? And where did you feel you were your true self, as in the very most authentic you at your best?

These are your victories, and they call for celebration! Write them down! Record them in your journal. You deserve to see the best in yourself and in your accomplishments. You deserve to tap into the power you feel as you triumph. Our daughter has four-year-old twins, and when they see me struggling with something, they will tell me, "You can do hard things, Gammie!" I love that they notice, and I love that they are learning that mindset.

Once you have written those victories down, it's time to look at results that you are NOT pleased with. When did you have expectations that did not become reality for you? When did you stop short of your goal and give up on the achievement?

In the book *Think and Grow Rich*, Napoleon Hill told the true story of a man who went to Colorado during the gold rush and bought a gold mine. He spent thousands of dollars on equipment so he could harvest the gold. He worked at the mine for many months until he finally quit. He sold all of his machinery and equipment for pennies on the dollar to a "junk dealer." The junk dealer consulted with an engineer, who told him to use the equipment and he would find gold if he just kept going. By continuing to dig, the junk dealer found a rich vein of gold just 3 feet from where the previous miner had stopped.

Worthwhile decisions almost always compel us to difficult actions. Most people give up when the going gets tough. Most people lose sight of their goal and allow uncertainty, fear, lack of self-confidence, and any number of excuses to prevent them from getting the results they want. Just so you know, we all have that tendency! It's way easier to avoid change.

If we use the analogy of a baby's diaper, avoiding change is not a comfortable way to live. Our comfort zone is something we are used to, familiar, easy, and predictable. It is the step outside the comfort zone that leads us into the Miracle Zone.

"We can't be afraid of change. You may feel very secure in the pond that you are in, but if you never venture out of it, you will never know that there is such a thing as an ocean, a sea. Holding onto something that is good for you now, may be the very reason why you don't have something better." C. JoyBell

When we start out with great intentions, we have momentum and a plan. We are excited! We can envision the great results we will have as we change our lives and move toward the goal! But it is a big challenge to keep that purpose foremost in our minds, especially when challenges come, as inevitably they will.

If we have given way to beliefs that hold us back, often called "limiting beliefs," we might hit the rock wall and not hang onto the notion that success is just three feet away. Even when we KNOW it's there, the last three feet can be really hard.

Divine wisdom tells us not to be weary in doing well, for we are building a strong foundation, our great legacy. It is out of small things that great things come.

Mighty change takes place with movement, with consistent action. The action doesn't have to be large, but it does have to be purposeful. We can't allow small distractions to pull us off course. Continuing forward with action toward your goal eliminates the power of the roadblock before you. Roy T. Bennett said, *"It's never too late to change your life for the better. You don't have to take huge steps to change your life. Making even the smallest changes to your daily routine can make a big difference to your life."*

What if you DON'T make the changes to take you to your better results? We can spend wasted time complaining about the obstacles, the difficulties, that challenges, the pain of change.

Maya Angelou said,
"There were people who went to sleep last night,
poor and rich and white and black,
but they will never wake again.
And those dead folks would give anything at all
for just five minutes of this weather
or ten minutes of plowing.
So you watch yourself about complaining.
What you're supposed to do
when you don't like a thing is change it.
If you can't change it,
change the way you think about it."

George Bernard Shaw said,
"Those who cannot change their minds cannot change any-
thing."

As you look at the results you are seeing in your life, how are you doing? Are you happy? Are you disappointed? Where in between? We can look around us or read about the results others have experienced, based upon the decisions they have made, and we can use our observations to help us with the decisions we make going forward.

What if today is an "off" day, and you can't get yourself going? Well, you are human, and there will be days like that. But even on the off days you can think ahead to tasks that fulfill your purpose but are not as demanding as days when you have full energy and are ready to tackle the world. Sometimes it is just a matter of "mind over mattress," as Stephen Covey said. Ezra Taft Benson said, "*Some of the greatest battles will be fought within the silent chambers of your own soul.*"

This morning I did many of the "right" things, but I couldn't get myself into the mode of taking purposeful action. I meditated and prayed, got dressed, made the bed, did some laundry, explored some things on the internet, read some things, drank some water, checked social media and my email and the news, all while telling myself that I was making important decisions about what to include in this chapter to make it more helpful to my tribe.

But the trajectory of my decisions was not leading to my desired end results. It was leading to a place of dissatisfaction, a place well within my comfort zone, where very little progress actually takes place. Oh, I can talk about what I want to do all day long, but it is putting plans into purposeful action that makes the difference.

When we REALLY THINK about what we want to accomplish, and THOUGHTFULLY write down our desired end results, and set out on our course of action that leads to the destination we desire, we can achieve what others might think is impossible.

Walt Disney said, "*It's kind of fun to do the impossible.*" Just look at what his vision and purposeful action created!

This thought fills my heart with smiles. It describes the motivation behind all of our efforts to achieve life changes that are filled with joy, on purpose. Walter Mosley: "*We are not trapped or locked up in these bones. No, no. We are free to change. And love changes us. And if we can love one another, we can break open the sky.*"

Chapter 30: When Your Mess Is Your Stress

Like many of you, we are becoming more minimalist with our possessions. Our time has been spent recently putting away gifts, sorting through things that needed to be sent on to a new home, figuring out what to eliminate, both in possessions and in our time commitments, to make room.

The vacuum law of prosperity states that if you create an empty space, it will fill. In order to attract something you want in your life, you have to make room for it. Inevitably, it will come, if you make space, move toward what you want, and then be patient.

So what I want in my life is a pretty tall order, and I'm willing to be REALLY patient for it to come. I have to make space for it in how I allocate my time, because it will require my working to bring the funds to make it happen. And there are other, much more urgent needs, that need to be filled as well.

As we look around at all the "stuff" that surrounds us, there simply isn't room to be a minimalist and still find a home for it all in one place. Games, projects, clothing, food, décor . . . it all needs to be put SOMEWHERE, and since we downsized a few years ago, the somewhere isn't as obvious as it was before. Our time, and our space, are cluttered.

Clutter creates stress! And stress is not a healthy option for our bodies or our minds. Interestingly, my husband, who is a medical doctor who specializes in helping people deal with the ravages of stress, says that oxidative stress is at the root of ALL degenerative diseases. That's a pretty good reason to get rid of stress!

Psychology Today says this about clutter:

Clutter bombards our minds with excessive stimuli (visual, olfactory, tactile), causing our senses to work overtime on stimuli that aren't necessary or important.

Clutter distracts us by drawing our attention away from what our focus should be on.

Clutter makes it more difficult to relax, both physically and mentally.

Clutter constantly signals to our brains that our work is never done.

Clutter makes us anxious because we're never sure what it's going to take to get through to the bottom of the pile.

Clutter creates feelings of guilt ("I should be more organized") and embarrassment, especially when others unexpectedly drop by our homes or work spaces.

Clutter inhibits creativity and productivity by invading the open spaces that allow most people to think, brainstorm, and problem solve.

Clutter frustrates us by preventing us from locating what we need quickly (e.g., files and paperwork lost in the "pile" or keys swallowed up by the clutter).

Clutter is the springboard for such quotes as "Out of clutter, find simplicity," and "Don't own so much clutter that you will be relieved to see your house catch fire."

When we think of clutter, we usually think about the "stuff" that surrounds us in the home or apartment where we live. And it's interesting to note we use the word "stuff" to talk about clutter. When we eat too much, we say we are "stuffed." The two uses of "stuff" have quite similar meanings.

"I don't like to brag or anything," says Eve Schuab in the Year of No Clutter—"but I really am exceptionally gifted when it comes to the "Stuff" department. If I had a title, it might be "Her Royal Highness, the Queen of Crap." I could look snootily down from high atop my pile of ancient magazines, holding a scepter of dried bridesmaid bouquets, bedecked with a crown made entirely of those extra button packs that helpfully accompany sweater purchases, proclaiming "SAVE IT!" in an emphatic yet regal tone."

Clutter can be physical "stuff" that surrounds and overwhelms us, but it can also be clutter that fills our minds with inconsequential tasks. We can clutter our schedules with activities that keep us busy, but don't move us toward our single most important objective. We can clutter our time and attention with social media excess, and with constant glances at our phone. Clutter and "stuff" can hold us back from achieving our dreams.

Monika Kristofferson says, *"Clutter steals energy and joy."*

The theme for my podcast is Joy on Purpose. Stepping into our Miracle Zone requires living a less complex, more purposeful life. If clutter steals our energy and joy, that doesn't get us any closer to our purpose, does it?

Just thinking about minimizing our excessive possessions can be overwhelming. But as Lisa Schultz said, *"My choice of a lighter lifestyle has brought me a greater sense of well-being. In a world that often seems stressful and chaotic, that's a feeling I cherish."*

You may have noticed that people who lived during the Great Depression and World War II have a greater tendency to hold onto "things." That was a time of war and scarcity, and many people did not have enough to eat, or a place to stay. Families went without. Folks struggled to find work. The result of that time lingers for those who suffered.

But while we should be prudent and save for a rainy day, so to speak, we don't need to clutter our lives and our minds with "stuff" that isn't going to add to our joy. I'm talking about papers we plan to read "someday," or small gifts or trinkets that fill our space but not our soul.

The acronym of the state "OHIO" also applies to items and deciding what to do with them: Only Handle It Once. That means when a bill comes, either pay it immediately and file the receipt, or you can do what I do, which is pay it and then put the receipts in an attractive basket. I sort through the basket and file the receipts about three times a year. Decision time is when you pick the paper up. You only handle it once.

Are you hanging onto clothes that either fit you once, or

you hope will fit you someday, or maybe come back into style from back when you were in sixth grade (and you're now in your forties)? Maybe now's a good time to say goodbye to the stuff that clutters your closet. Maybe now's a good time to say goodbye to the six pizza cutters, the dozen different spatulas, and the mismatched glasses.

Think how much your unneeded stuff could bless someone who doesn't have those items and cannot afford them. Giving them to thrift stores can help people get a new start when they have very little.

Here's a tip to help you with your master plan for decluttering your life and your home: Get Centered! Getting centered means deciding who you are, what you plan for, what is important to you, and what you need to accomplish your goals. Too much of any type of thing can confuse and distract you from your purpose.

So here's what I mean when I suggest you Get Centered: You create centers in your home, and you plan the contents of each center to be items that go with your center plan. For example: in your garage, you might have a car care center, a cleaning center, a gardening center, and a tool center. Make sure when you plan your space to allocate sufficient storage for each item in the center it belongs to. If you have more than fits, you either have to reassign the space or get rid of the excess.

Do the same in your kitchen. Decide what centers you need. You can have a baking center, a snack center, a center for your silverware and your plates that is nearest the dining table, a spice center, and a food prep center. Each area is designed with how many items should go into that space. You can do the same with your closets, your library, your basement, . . . and your Self.

That's right. You need to start all of this transformational process by getting centered in your head, with who you are, what is important to you, and what you are going to fit into your overall plan for your life. Some call it their "bucket list," but I prefer to call it my "live-it list."

It's not going to be fast, and it's not going to be easy, to get yourself to a place of less clutter, and a more purposeful life. But, although it may sound cliché, the joy is in the journey. You can fuel your enthusiasm by observing how wonderful it feels to be more in control, less stressed, and happier than you were when your mess was your stress.

"*In a world of people who are self-centered, become the Centered Self.*"--Cristie Gardner. You have to become very clear about what you want to do and be.

Michael Porter said, "*The essence of strategy is choosing what not to do.*" I've written in previous chapters about getting rid of the extraneous time fillers that don't bring us joy. Lee Bolman said, "*A vision without a strategy remains an illusion.*" Let's be more intentional about what we want and prioritize this precious life so we come to the end knowing we have reached a place of Joy on Purpose.

Jenkin Lloyd Jones summed it up nicely when he said, "*Anyone who imagines that bliss is normal is going to waste a lot of time running around shouting that he has been robbed. The fact is that most putts don't drop, most beef is tough, most children grow up to be just like people, most successful marriages require a high degree of mutual toleration, and most jobs are more often dull than otherwise. Life is just like an old time rail journey . . . delays, sidetracks, smoke, dust, cinders, and jolts, interspersed only occasionally by beautiful vistas and thrilling bursts of speed. The trick is to thank the Lord for letting you have the ride."*

And that, my friends, is

Stepping out of your Comfort Zone . . . and into Your Miracle Zone.

Cristie Gardner loves people and is a POWERHOUSE as a teacher and trainer.

As a Miracle Activator and Life Coach, she coaches and mentors with love, wisdom and life-transforming insight.

As a speaker, she received top regional honors in Toastmasters.

As a mother and homemaker, she raised eight—yes, eight—amazing children, who are all grown, and effective leaders in their own right.

She is **passionate about travel** and wants to see all of the countries in the world (not just as a tourist—she wants to KNOW the people and their countries).

Life, for her, is about manifesting dreams through conscious, consistent effort, love, gratitude, resilience, and a lot of faith.

0 - 9823 39 9 - 0

CPSIA information can be obtained
at www.ICGtesting.com
Printed in the USA
BVHW031113071021
618237BV00007B/10